WITNESS

WRITINGS OF
BARTOLOMÉ DE LAS CASAS

D1118218

WITNESS

WRITINGS OF
BARTOLOMÉ DE LAS CASAS

Edited and translated by
George Sanderlin

with a Foreword by
Gustavo Gutiérrez

ORBIS BOOKS
Maryknoll, New York 10545

Second Printing, January 1993

The Catholic Foreign Mission Society of America (Maryknoll) recruits and trains people for overseas missionary service. Through Orbis Books, Maryknoll aims to foster the international dialogue that is essential to mission. The books published, however, reflect the opinions of their authors and are not meant to represent the official position of the society.

Published in 1992 by Orbis Books, Maryknoll, NY 10545 by arrangement with Alfred A. Knopf, Inc.

Manufactured in the United States of America

Foreword by Gustavo Gutiérrez was translated by Robert R. Barr.

Selections from Bartolomé de Las Casas, *Del Unico Modo de Atraer a Todos los Pueblos a la Verdadera Religión*, ed. Augustín Millares Carlo (Mexico City: Fondo de Cultura Económica, 1942) are reprinted by permission.

Library of Congress Cataloging-in-Publication Data

Casas, Bartolomé de las, 1474-1566.
  [Selections. English. 1992]
  Witness : writings of Bartolomé de las Casas / edited and
translated by George Sanderlin ; with a foreword by Gustavo
Gutiérrez.
    p. cm.
  Originally published: Bartolomé de las Casas. New York : Knopf,
[1971].
  Includes bibliographical references.
  Contents: pt. 1. Historian—pt. 2. Autobiographer—pt.
3. Anthropologist—pt. 4. Political thinker.
  ISBN 0-88344-790-8 (pbk.)
    1. America—Discovery and exploration—Spanish. 2. Indians,
Treatment of—Latin America. 3. Spain—Colonies—America.
  I. Sanderlin, George William, 1915- . II. Title.
F1411.C4273 1992
970.01'6—dc20
                                              91-30348
                                              CIP

Contents

**PART I
HISTORIAN**

v

PART II
AUTOBIOGRAPHER

PART III
ANTHROPOLOGIST

PART IV
POLITICAL THINKER

Publisher's Foreword

There is a great need in 1992 for an anthology of the work of Bartolomé de Las Casas. This was recognized three years ago by Lewis Hanke, the dean of twentieth-century Las Casas scholars, but his illness in 1990 caused him to abandon the project. The world was left with a major figure, Bartolomé de Las Casas, who has been mentioned more and more during the approach of the Quincentenary, but most often as the author of a single pamphlet (though his complete works are now being published in fourteen volumes) and as a denouncer of atrocities. Yet he worked for fifty years on behalf of the Indians — as reformer, statesman, legislator, and publicist, and is now being viewed as the father of American history and anthropology, and as an early proponent of democracy and even a form of the United Nations.

So rather than let the Quincentenary come and go with no Las Casas anthology at all, Orbis is reprinting the anthology produced in 1971 by George Sanderlin under the guidance of Lewis Hanke. To be sure, there are some caveats. But, at the very least, the general reader can have a bowing acquaintance (better, a "reading acquaintance") with Bartolomé de Las Casas, the historical personage who best answers the current debate over 1492 — should we celebrate or should we weep?

Obviously, an anthology compiled twenty-five years ago does not necessarily reflect current scholarship. In recounting the life of Las Casas, sketched in the Introduction, George Sanderlin relied on the work of the late Giménez Fernández, once considered an "authoritative biographer," but seen now as having been prone to conjecture. Such errors have been eliminated from Sanderlin's text when there is well-known evidence to the contrary; when the correction is from a new or forthcoming book, that is signalled in an Editor's note. As for Las Casas' writings, Sanderlin makes no mention of Las Casas' last major books—those on royal power and on Peru. These have been added to the Bibliography, along with new reference works on Fray Bartolomé, and additional books soon to be published.

Nonetheless, Sanderlin's anthology is a valuable introduction. During all the fervor of the Quincentary, which has seen both the resurfacing of calumnies against Las Casas, as well as impassioned defenses, this anthology presents Las Casas not as the caricatured author of one pamphlet, the "Brevissima," but as an important literary figure, a Christian prophet, and a thoughtful political theorist. That Las Casas is a backdrop against which the reader can watch the progressive rediscovery of a dynamic "new Las Casas" who will undoubtedly emerge during the coming years.

—The Editors

❧ Foreword ❧

The Indian: Person and Poor

The Theological Perspective of Bartolomé de Las Casas

GUSTAVO GUTIÉRREZ

Among those with the keenest interest in Bartolomé de Las Casas today are Latin America's liberation theologians, who have recognized in the Dominican friar a prophetic forerunner of the church's radical "option for the poor." Among the best-known exponents of this theology is Gustavo Gutiérrez, a Peruvian priest who works with the poor in Lima and is associated with the Instituto Bartolomé de Las Casas. His many books include A Theology of Liberation, The God of Life, *and, most recently,* Las Casas: In Search of the Poor of Jesus Christ.

For a full nineteen years, the inhabitants of the so-called West Indies had suffered occupation, mistreatment, exploitation, and death at the hands of those who, from their European viewpoint, considered themselves the discoverers of these lands. The newcomers dealt with the Indians, says Las Casas, "as if they had been good-for-nothing animals," since they only sought to "grow rich on the blood of those poor wretches." This induced the Dominican religious of Hispaniola to combine "rights with facts" ("el derecho con el hecho") — to combine their reflection with a knowledge of the situation, and to confront the oppression they saw there with the "law of Christ."

The Dominican friars delegated to one of their number, Antón Montesino, the task of making this denunciation, which he performed in his sermon for the Fourth Sunday of Advent, 1511. Let us reproduce here the passage that Fray Bartolomé cites verbatim from that sermon:

> You are all in mortal sin, and live and die in it, because of the cruelty and tyranny you practice among these innocent peoples. Tell me, by what right or justice do you hold these Indians in such a cruel and horrible servitude? . . . And what care do you take that they should be instructed in religion, so that they may know their God and creator, may be baptized, may hear Mass, and may keep Sunday and feast days? (See p. 67.)

The friars go even further, with Montesino as their spokesperson. To these denunciations they add the foundation of what was to yield a distinct characteristic. The Indians are persons. Consequently they have all of the rights of persons. "Are these not human beings?" Then they recall the demand of the gospel: "Are you not bound to love them as you love yourselves? Don't you understand this?" They were enunciating something radically required of any Christian: an acceptance of the equality of persons, including Spaniards and Indians, before God ("as yourselves"), and then — over and above the demands of justice, which were being so perfidiously violated — leaping to the categories of love, which knows no juridical or philosophical limits. This evangelical perspective, it seems to me, is the key to an understanding of the challenge issued by the Dominicans.

Thus was posed, as clearly as could be, a central question, and one that will be debated long and passionately. Who is the Indian? Who, for the Europeans, is the dweller of the so-called New World? Actually, the matter divides into two great questions: Who are the Indians from the viewpoint of their human condition? And who are the Indians, considered from a religious perspective? Answers will vary. Among them, the most original and most evangelical is that of Bartolomé de Las Casas.

Human Condition of the Indian

Ever since they began having contact with the Indians, Europeans arriving here regarded them as inferior beings. We find this attitude in the descriptions written by Christopher Columbus himself, only to worsen with the passing years, as the Indians were treated more and more callously. Soon, theories would be formulated concerning their human condition. As Las Casas puts it, it was their treatment in practice as "irrational beasts" that was the "cause of the doubt in the minds of persons who had never seen them as to whether they were human beings or animals." Two clear, opposite positions now took shape.

Two Classes of Human Beings

As the sixteenth century opens, we find an important theologian in Paris among the first to speak of the inferiority of the American person. We refer to the Scotsman John Major, who cites Aristotle in support of his ideas. In an attempt to justify the European conquest of the Indies, Major writes:

The first persons to occupy those lands may by right govern the tribes that inhabit them. In Books I, III, and IV of the *Politics*, the Philosopher states that there can be no doubt that some are by nature slaves and others free, that this is inescapably to the advantage of some, and that it is just that some should command and others obey, and that in [the matter of] dominion, which is as it were connatural, one must command, and therefore dominate, and another obey.

The battle lines were drawn. Some are born to slaveholding, others to slavery. It is all a matter of nature. Accordingly, Europeans may licitly exercise dominion over the inhabitants of the

Indies. And not only may they do so, but they must—for the very benefit of these lesser beings. Philosophy and theology, then, find themselves in the service of European imperialism. Let us not imagine that we are dealing with an isolated position. The ideas expounded by Major in Paris will be in evidence in Burgos, too, when—due to the protest of the Hispaniola Dominicans—the first laws of the Indies will be discussed in 1512. Spanish theologians of note will maintain the same theses as their Scots colleague.

Let us limit ourselves to a consideration of the most vehement and best known representative of this line of thinking: Ginés de Sepúlveda. Here we have a most bitter adversary of Las Casas, and one with whom the latter maintained a heated polemic in Valladolid until 1550. Sepúlveda was a leading authority on, and translator of, Aristotle, and like Major, appealed to "the Philosopher" as one of his sources. The Spanish humanist explains:

> With perfect right do the Spanish exercise their dominion over these barbarians of the New World and outlying isles, who in prudence, natural disposition, and every manner of virtue and human sentiment are as inferior to Spaniards as children to adults, women to men, cruel and inhuman persons to the extremely meek, or the exceedingly intemperate to the continent and moderate—in a word, as monkeys to men.

Those born to be slaves must be subjected to those destined to dominate. This will be one of the justifying reasons for the wars against the Indians. The purpose of these wars is regarded as the guarantee that they are waged "with rectitude, justice, and piety, and that, while affording some utility to the people that conquer, they provide a much greater benefit to the barbarians that are conquered." The Indians gain in humanity by being subjugated to the Europeans, even by means of war.

To be sure, these expressions and notions shock us. But we must at least give them credit for honesty. There are still persons today whose discourse is egalitarian enough, but whose practice demonstrates a similar contempt for non-European races and cultures.

All Human Beings Are Equal

Las Casas is a fierce champion of the equality of all human beings. It is something of which he is deeply convinced, and he refers to it over and over again. One of his most important works, the *Apologética Histórica*, is devoted to demonstrating the integrally human condition of the Indians. He tells us of the social, cultural, artistic, and ethical achievements of the native populations. The guiding thread in this description—which is one of the most important sources of our knowledge of the old civilizations of the Indies—is expounded in passages like this one:

> All the nations of the world are made up of human beings, and of each and every human being there is one definition and one only: that they are rational. [This means that] all have their understanding and will and their free choice, inasmuch as they are fashioned to the image and likeness of God. . . . All have the natural principles or germinal capacity to understand and to learn, and to know the sciences and things that they know not.

There are not two classes of human beings, then. Rather, all of us have been made to the image and likeness of God. We all have reason, will, and free choice. We are all fundamentally equal. To this forthright declaration of human equality, Las Casas adds a no-less-determined defense of freedom. He writes, in one of his treatises:

> From their very origin, all rational creatures are born free—inasmuch as, in one equal nature, God has not made us slaves of one another but has granted to all an identical [freedom of] choice. Therefore one rational creature is not subordinate to another, as, for example, one human being to another, seeing that freedom is a right present in human beings necessarily and *per se*, in virtue of the very principle of the rational creature. Therefore it [freedom] is a natural right.

The thesis is clear. The Spanish Dominican takes a position diametrically opposed to the one we have examined in the foregoing section, which is that some persons must of necessity be subject to others. According to Las Casas, Europeans and Indians share one and the same human nature. Consequently he rejects the claim that wars may be legitimately waged for the purpose of gaining dominion over the Indian nations. Instead, he demands respect for the cultures, customs, and even religions of the native peoples.

Being free and equal, the Indians have a right to the ownership of goods. Those are in grievous error, then, who think that they may be deprived of such. For the same reason, the native political authorities that govern these lands are legitimate, and therefore ought to be respected by all. The Indies are not a "no man's land." Indeed, Europeans may not remain on this continent unless the Indians accept that presence. In two bold tractates, Las Casas postulates: "No subjection, no servitude, no task may be imposed on the people to be burdened with the same unless that people give its free consent to such imposition." The popular will must prevail even over that of the rulers of a given society: "The kings, princes, elders, and high functionaries who have imposed taxes and tribute have done so by virtue of the free consent of the people, and all of their authority, power, and jurisdiction has come to them through the popular will." Las Casas' forthright defense of democracy has its roots in certain currents of medieval thought, as well as in his personal experience as a member of the Dominican Order.

His conviction of the equality of all human beings, and his vigorous proclamation of the Indians' right to be free, are the twin pillars of Las Casas' philosophical anthropology. One of Bartolomé's strengths is that he is not afraid to go wherever his theology and his conscience may dictate. How simple. And yet how difficult for so many.

Salvation in Christ

The conquest and colonization of the Indies was quickly presented in Europe as a missionary endeavor. The salvation of the new infidels, through their incorporation into the church, was to be the primary motive advanced to justify the European presence on this continent. The proclamation of salvation in Jesus Christ constitutes Las Casas' great concern, as well, and thus is the basic reason for his own missionary effort. Naturally this involves the question of the religious status of those who will receive the gospel message. Here again, two great responses present themselves.

Infidels and Idolaters

From the outset, missionaries to the Indies had wondered: To what class of infidel did the inhabitants of these lands belong? Were they hearing the gospel for the first time? Had the gospel been preached before, so that therefore they must have rejected it? What was the difference between them and the Muslims—the infidels to whom the Spaniards were most accustomed? One thing was sure: they were infidels. Furthermore they were idolaters: not only had they not received faith in Christ, they worshiped false gods to boot. Here, as well as with regard to the precise nature of this idolatry, various opinions prevailed.

The subject was not merely theoretical. While some of the responses given to these conundrums were exotic ones, all were laden with practical consequences in terms of how the Indians were to be treated. The most important concerned the licitness and legitimacy of wars of conquest as a means of evangelization, along with the ensuing domination. Many were the theologians (Ginés de Sepúlveda among them), and even missioners, who saw no other way of Christianizing these peoples whom they regarded as inferior, recalcitrant, and unteachable.

Bartolomé, for his part, regarded it as scandalous and sacrilegious to preach the gospel by means of death-dealing wars and exploitation. In his first book, he propounds a thesis that he will spend the rest of his life defending:

The one and only method of teaching men the true religion was established by Divine Providence for the whole world, and for all times, that is, by persuading the understanding through reasons, and by gently attracting or exhorting the will. This method should be common to all men throughout the world, without any distinction made for sects, errors, or corrupt customs. (See p. 138.)

The manner of evangelization Las Casas proposes is an expression of respect for the freedom of the Indians—in this case, freedom of religion. War is radically contrary to the spirit and letter of the message of Jesus.

On the point of respect for the religious customs of the Indians, Las Casas holds a very firm position. Let us see, for example, the most difficult and delicate situation that he had to face: that of the human sacrifice and cannibalism that had been discovered among some Indian nations. Sixteenth-century Europeans were speechless with horror. Our Dominican friar makes a daring effort to understand this behavior from within the Indians' religious world. His reasoning is as follows. Any religious person seeks to offer God the most valuable thing in his or her possession. But surely human life is the most precious thing we have. Consequently, says Las Casas—generating chills, of course, in his hearers and readers—"unless some human or divine positive law forbids them to do so, and in the absence of grace or doctrine, as human beings they are obliged to offer to the true God, or to the one they consider to be the true God, human sacrifices."

Obviously there is no question of approving such sacrifices. Las Casas rejects them out of hand. He is only attempting to understand why certain Indian peoples went so far as to perform them. One of the great efforts of our friar was to see things from within the Indian world. Here, the result is a profound respect for the religious customs of the Indians, and for their religious freedom.

Scourged Christs

For Las Casas, salvation in Christ is strictly bound up with the establishment of social justice. The bond is so important for him that it leads him, on two important points, to invert the hierarchy of problems traditionally posed by missionaries. Fray

Bartolomé regards the main question as that of the salvation of the Spaniards themselves, and not only that of the infidel Indians. Those who claim to be Christians must cease from their robbery and exploitation of the Indians, else they will surely be condemned: "for it is impossible that anyone be saved without observing justice." In other words, the salvation of the "faithful" is at greater risk than that of the "infidels." This is at the root of the task Las Casas takes upon himself with regard to the "faithful."

Furthermore, with prophetic insight, he sees in the Indians more the evangelical "poor" than infidels. And so he writes to Charles V of Spain that if the evangelization of the Indians means "their death and total destruction, as has been the case until now, it would not be unsuitable that Your Majesty should cease to be their lord, and that they had never been Christians." That is, an "infidel, but living, Indian" is of greater value than a "Christian, but dead, Indian." Here, on the basis of the gospel, Bartolomé calls into question the whole religious and social order being imposed in the Indies. Las Casas so energetically defends the value of human life, including physical life, because for him physical life, too, is a precious gift of God.

We must not think, however, that Las Casas sees in the Indian only the poor—those favorite persons of the God of the Reign. Surely this was his primary intuition. But he gradually perceives the injustices that victimize blacks (many of them Muslims), *guanches* (inhabitants of the Canary Islands), and even the Spanish poor.*

---

*There is a stubborn misperception in this area, and it is time it was laid to rest. In 1516, Las Casas, like all of his contemporaries, supported a petition that slaves, "black or white," be transported to the Antilles to relieve the plight of the Indians there. This intervention on his part has given rise to the mistaken notion that Las Casas caused the first black slaves to be brought to the Indies. This is not true. Black slaves had accompanied the Spaniards in their first voyages. Furthermore, as early as 1501 a royal order had legalized the ignominious traffic in black slaves. But most importantly, it is forgotten that Las Casas has left us clear, painful testimonials of his grief over the unfortunate opinion he held in his early struggles in behalf of the Indian. In his *History of the Indies*, the work he labored on most intensively and most at length, he indignantly rejects the fashion in which the Portuguese made slaves among the black peoples of Africa, with their lawless, immoral incursions on that continent. As he gained

However, there can be no doubt that his great concern was for the fate of the vast majority of the inhabitants of these lands, the Indies, whom he saw dying in wars, oppression, and illness. The root of his strong position, and the basis of its full meaning, lies in his fertile christological outlook.

From the very outset of his battle, Las Casas had gained a clear awareness that the oppression of the Indian is contrary to the "intention of Jesus Christ and of the whole of Scripture." What God wishes is rather the "liberation of the oppressed." This conviction was deeply rooted in our Dominican missioner, and it constituted a driving force in the struggle he was to wage for the rest of his life. The poor are God's favorite persons because, says Las Casas, "of the least and most forgotten, God has an altogether fresh and vivid memory." This preference, then, ought to be a norm of life for the Christian. And reminding us that those who exploit and murder the Indian do so "first and foremost for gold," Bartolomé excoriates the perpetrators of this evil, saying, "Christ did not come into the world to die for gold." On the contrary, it will be gold, money, ambition for wealth, and capital that will put Christ to death, by murdering the Indians, the poor. On one of his most profound, most beautiful, and most evangelical pages, the Dominican friar will identify the "Indian oppressed" with Christ himself.

In his *History of the Indies*, Las Casas tells us of his effort, shortly after his conversion, to "come to the rescue of this wretched folk, and stay their perishing." It was now that he embarked on the difficult and questionable enterprise of a peaceful colonization in the territory of today's Venezuela. To this purpose, he paid the King money in exchange for the concession of lands and other considerations.

These negotiations scandalized someone who thought very

---

familiarity with that phenomenon, he changed his way of thinking, and perceived that to subject blacks to slavery was a profound and scandalous injustice. The reason was that it violated basic human rights: "Blacks," he says, "have the same right to liberty as Indians." Furthermore, he declares, as to his statement in 1516, that he "is not sure whether his ignorance and good intention will exonerate him before the judgment seat of God." Paradoxically, then, the judgment of historians is that Las Casas was the first person in the sixteenth century to denounce black slavery as inhumane and unjust.

highly of the cleric Las Casas, who favored his admirer with an explanation. The reply in question constitutes one of the most impressive passages of his entire work. *"I leave in the Indies,"* he says, *"Jesus Christ,* our God, scourged and afflicted and beaten and crucified *not once, but thousands of times,* when the Spaniards devastate and destroy its peoples."

Hence Bartolomé's conviction that, if you love Christ, you will do your best to free the Indians, and to prevent their being "deprived of life before their time" through the regime of the *encomienda,* or royal bestowal of lands and their inhabitants on the colonists. Indeed, Las Casas identifies the Indians with Christ. Thus he manifests an acute sense of the poor, and of the concrete, material, temporal life of the poor. To despoil them, exploit them, kill them, is to "blaspheme the name of Christ."

There are echos of this biblical notion (cf. Rom. 2:24) in another work of Fray Bartolomé de Las Casas. Writing on the subject of the bond between love for God and love for neighbor, Las Casas explicitly cites Matthew 25, the Parable of the Last Judgment. "God takes as done to himself," he observes, "the deeds done in ministry discharged on behalf of his servant." What is done to or for the poor reaches beyond them, to God present in them. A few pages further on, he cites Augustine's trenchant question: "If, then, that one must go to eternal fire to whom Christ says, 'I was naked and you did not clothe me,' what will be the lot of the one to whom he says, 'I was clothed and you stripped me naked'?" Because this is what is actually happening in the Indies. There, not only are the naked not clothed, but the poor are wretchedly, violently stripped even of what they have. They are despoiled of what is theirs by right. The poor, and, in them, Christ himself, are plundered.

This outlook is obviously beyond the grasp of those who regard the Indians as a naturally inferior race, like Las Casas' great adversary Ginés de Sepúlveda (or his sophisticated followers today). Nor indeed is it available to those who see in these natives only the depositories of rights formally equal to those of everyone else, but who fail to look beyond, like Francisco de Vitoria. We reach this pinnacle of spirituality only if, like Bartolomé de Las Casas, we perceive the Indians as the poor of the gospel.

And here we plumb to the core of Las Casas' theological thought. Yes, the dwellers of the Indies are persons, equal to Europeans, human beings with all of the rights thereunto appertaining. But more than this, for Las Casas they are "our brothers and sisters, and Christ has given his life for them" to the point of identifying himself with these "Indian oppressed." Las Casas had the perspicacity, and the daring, to see the Indian as more than an infidel, more than a non-Christian. He looked more closely, and saw someone poor, in the gospel sense. His life and work can only be understood from a point of departure in this germinal intuition. It is in the light of this intuition that the pages to follow should be read.

Lima, 1992

WITNESS

WRITINGS OF
BARTOLOMÉ DE LAS CASAS

Introduction

Bartolomé de Las Casas (1484-1566) spent a lifetime challenging the justice of Spanish conduct in the New World. For over fifty years after his decision in 1514 to defend the Indians, Las Casas carried on his crusade for Indian rights—the first important campaign for an underprivileged group in the Americas.

During his campaign, Las Casas dramatized the plight of the Indians in his sensational *Very Brief Account of the Destruction of the Indies*; helped secure the passage of the New Laws in 1542, which effected fundamental reforms; brought the machine of conquest itself to a grinding halt in 1550 while the Emperor Charles V pondered Las Casas' charges of injustice; and found time to write not only innumerable treatises and memorials but also masterpieces of history, anthropology, and applied theology. The historian Samuel Eliot Morison has called Las Casas' *History of the Indies* "the one book on the discovery of America that I should wish to preserve if all others were destroyed."[1]

Las Casas' life extended through the first seventy-four years of Spanish discovery and conquest of the New World. Indeed, Las Casas took a *pars magna* in the astounding events by which Spain claimed an empire stretching from Canada to the Strait of Magellan. He crossed the Atlantic ten times, sailed the Pacific, participated in the conquest of Cuba, converted warlike natives of Guatemala, attended church conferences in Mexico City, and fought for the Indians before New World *audiencias* and, above all, at the peripatetic Spanish court.

Among those he observed or knew well, as friends or foes, were Christopher Columbus, Bishop Juan Rodríguez de Fonseca, Diego Columbus, Ferdinand Columbus, Ferdinand and Isabella, Bartholomew Columbus, Diego Velázquez, Ximénez

1

de Cisneros, Ponce de León, Charles V, Philip II, Vasco Núñez
Balboa, Antonio Montesino, Ferdinand Magellan, Bernal Díaz
del Castillo, Gonzalo Fernández de Oviedo, and Hernando Cortés—to name but a few. His cell in the Dominican monastery at
Valladolid was a kind of archive of the Americas, containing
among other documents an abstract made by Las Casas of
Columbus' *Journal*, the only version of the *Journal* destined to
survive.

Bartolomé de las Casas was born in Seville in the latter part
of 1484; as he himself tells us, he was a descendant of "old
Christians" who had settled in that town. His father, Pedro, was
a merchant, and Las Casas had three sisters, one of whom married and died young. About his mother, nothing definite is
known. What is known is that the youthful Las Casas was deeply
affected by Columbus' discovery.

In April 1493, when he was only eight and a half, Bartolomé
saw Columbus passing through the streets of Seville on his triumphant return from his first voyage. The Admiral of the Ocean
Sea was accompanied by seven Indians bearing red and green
parrots, fishbone belts and masks, and samples of gold. In September 1493, Bartolomé's father and two uncles sailed with
Columbus on his second voyage. When Pedro returned to Seville
in 1498, he presented Bartolomé with a Taino Indian youth as
his servant. This youth was later freed by order of Queen Isabella and sent back to the Indies, but perhaps not before young
Bartolomé had been impressed by the Taino's gentle nature.

In January 1502, Bartolomé de Las Casas embarked for the
Indies in the fleet of Commander Nicolás de Ovando. Still a
teenager, he was apparently going to help in the family business,
which seems to have involved farming and trading. After an
uneventful passage, the ships anchored in Santo Domingo harbor, and Bartolomé heard his companions eagerly shouting to
their compatriots on shore, "What news? What news is there is
the land?"

"Good news, good news!" came the reply. "There is much
gold! A nugget was found weighing so many pounds—and there
is a war with the Indians, so there will be plenty of slaves!"[2]

The Indians being enslaved were the gentle, handsome, hos-
pitable Tainos. Columbus described their young men as "fairly

tall and good-looking, well built." Men and women went clad in loin cloths, or "quite naked, as their mothers bore them."³ They painted their faces, or their entire bodies, white, black, or red. Bartolomé would soon become familiar with their thatch huts, their utensils of shell, and their ineffectual and rarely used weapons—wooden darts with either fire-hardened ends or fish-tooth points. They had welcomed the white men joyously as gods; now, overworked and underfed in the damp mines or beneath the tropical sun, their balanced ecology disrupted, they were perishing.

But what was Bartolomé de Las Casas like when, at the age of eighteen, he first set foot in this marvelous New World? From his later success as a planter, he seems to have been ambitious and competent. An enemy, Gonzalo Fernández de Oviedo, said that Las Casas "wished to rule."⁴ The editor Juan Pérez de Tudela finds him preeminently a man of action—tenacious, courageous, with great foresight and self-confidence; at the same time, says Tudela, he was gifted with a fertile imagination, reasoning ability, scientific curiosity, and a remarkable memory.⁵ In later years, Las Casas showed his love for books by carrying his large library with him wherever he went, like St. Jerome, and on one occasion, following a shipwreck, dug many volumes out of the mud of the Yucatán coast.

"A person of choleric temperament, like the cleric"⁶—that is, passionate, energetic, quick to react—Las Casas says of himself, in the *History of the Indies*. He was a keen satirist although perhaps not a true humorist, according to Henry R. Wagner. We have no contemporary portrait of Las Casas, but from some sentences in Las Casas' *Apologetic History* Wagner infers that he was of medium height and olive complexion.⁷ He had an incredibly strong constitution.

In Hispaniola, Las Casas seems to have lived much like the other colonists—that is, like those of good character. There is no evidence he ever bore arms, though he did accompany punitive expeditions against "rebellious" Indians, most likely as a provisioner. For this, or for his family's loyalty to Columbus, he received an *encomienda* near La Concepción. An *encomienda* was a tract of land or village whose Indians were entrusted to a Spanish settler who, in return for instructing the Indians in

Christian doctrine – or promising to instruct them – had the right to their forced labor in fields and mines. In 1506-1507, Las Casas journeyed to Rome, where he was ordained a priest. He returned to Hispaniola around 1509, and in 1510 celebrated his first solemn High Mass at La Concepción, with Governor Diego Colón and his lady in the congregation. As Las Casas relates proudly in his *History*, it was "the first New Mass in all these Indies."[8]

In 1513, Las Casas accompanied Pánfilo de Narváez as a chaplain on the Spanish conquest of Cuba. He was again given a desirable encomienda, this time on the Arimao River in that island, by Governor Diego Velázquez. With the help of his partner, the pious Pedro de Rentería, Las Casas farmed, raised cattle, traded with Hispaniola and Puerto Rico, and prospered. But a great change was about to take place in his life.

Las Casas had always treated his Indians humanely. However, he became increasingly troubled by the cruelty of many of the other settlers. Partly from disease and partly from overwork and abuse, nine-tenths of the native population of Hispaniola had already disappeared. When the Dominicans under Prior Pedro de Córdoba had come to Hispaniola in 1510 and launched a campaign against mistreatment of the Indians, Las Casas had not been convinced by their arguments. (Once he wished to confess to a Dominican, and the friar refused to hear his confession because he held Indians.) But later, during the conquest of Cuba, upon witnessing the horrible massacre of Indians by Spaniards at Caonao, where he saw "a stream of blood running . . . as if a great number of cows had perished,"[9] Las Casas had tried in vain to stop the massacre of the Indians. By then, if he asked an Indian in any village how he fared, the Indian always replied, "Hungry, hungry, hungry."[10] The tragedy of Hispaniola was being repeated more swiftly and dramatically in Cuba.

In the spring of 1514, when he was thirty years old, Las Casas was preparing to preach the sermon for Pentecost at Espíritu Santo. He looked through the Bible for a text, and his eye fell on a passage from Ecclesiasticus 34, beginning: "Tainted his gifts who offers in sacrifice ill-gotten goods." For several days, he searched through Scripture and his own books of philosophy and law. And he concluded that "everything done to the Indians in these Indies was unjust and tyrannical," and "decided to preach that."[11]

First, he arranged to give up his own Indians, so he could speak freely against the encomienda. Then he made his sermon—delayed until the Feast of the Assumption, August 15, 1514—a denunciation of Spanish exploitation of the natives. He followed it with several others, which astonished but did not persuade his hearers. Las Casas realized that to achieve any reform, he would have to go back to Spain and see the king. The decision was approved by his partner, Rentería, who had reached a similar conclusion; by three Dominicans who came to Cuba in early 1515 and also preached to deaf ears; and finally, in Hispaniola, by Fray Pedro de Córdoba himself. Las Casas would lobby for stronger measure than the Laws of Burgos that had been enacted in 1512 in response to the Dominican complaints. Those provisions for better treatment of the Indians had been little heeded by the colonists, and, in any case, left the encomienda system intact. Las Casas immediately made this system his chief object of attack.

He arrived in Seville in October 1515 and had a brief audience with King Ferdinand in December, but the king died shortly after, before Las Casas could effectively state his case. Las Casas also saw Secretary Lope Conchillos, who offered him favors in the New World if he would call off his campaign; and bishop Juan Rodríguez de Fonseca, the wily overseer of Indian affairs, who listened impatiently to Las Casas' account of the Indians' sufferings and scornfully inquired, "What is that to me?"

"What is it to your lordship and to the king that those souls die?" retorted the "choleric" Las Casas. "Oh, great and eternal God! Who is there to whom that *is* something?"[12]

Las Casas then set out, undismayed, for Flanders, to protest to young Charles I. When he reached Madrid, he addressed memorials about the Indians to Cardinal Ximénez de Cisneros and Dean Adrian of Utrecht, co-regents of Spain. The austere cardinal advised Las Casas not to go on to Flanders; they would attend to his business in Spain.

This was a time of high hopes, not only for Las Casas but for all Europe. Men's imaginations were stirred by the voyages of

Christopher Columbus, Vasco da Gama, John Cabot, and others—by the wonders of the new lands. The threat of the Turk in the east seemed to be counterbalanced by the westward expansion. New ideas, inspired by recently discovered Greek manuscripts as well as by the voyages, were in the air, and the religious strife, wars, and economic decline of the second half of the century did not yet exist. Something of this buoyant optimism is reflected in Las Casas' programs for reform in the period 1516-1522.

Probably in Cuba he had sketched a "community scheme" to replace the encomienda system: Indians would be settled in villages of their own, grouped around a central Spanish town, and would work under a few carefully chosen Spanish supervisors but would share in the profits from their enterprises. Las Casas devised this utopia, with its elaborate welfare system, in 1515, the same year that Sir Thomas More wrote his *Utopia*. Then in 1516, Las Casas rewrote the plan in "court style" and it became the basis for the instructions of an Investigative Commission of Jeronymite friars sent to govern Hispaniola. Las Casas himself was appointed Protector of the Indians, and in 1516-1517 accompanied the Jeronymites to the West Indies, where they had been ordered by Cisneros to replace the encomiendas with supervised Indian villages if that were practicable. In 1518-1519, Las Casas attempted to recruit Spanish farmers who would emigrate to the Indies and help establish an integrated society of Spaniards and Indians working together, in place of Spanish masters exploiting Indian slaves. And in 1520, he obtained a grant of land in Venezuela, where he could found a colony and put his theories into practice.

Unfortunately, all these plans miscarried. Las Casas' Indian communities were not established. The Jeronymite committee, to his disgust, yielded to pressure from the colonists and retained the encomienda system. The effort to recruit Spanish peasants for the New World foundered on the determined opposition of large landowners who would not permit a drain on their labor force.[13]

This left the project for a colony in Venezuela, where Las Casas hoped to save the mainland Indians from the fate of the Tainos. In 1520, Charles I, just elected Holy Roman Emperor

Charles V, granted Las Casas 260 leagues (about 800 miles) of the coast, occupied only by Indians and a few missionaries. Las Casas promised a peaceful conversion of the Indians, the founding of five Spanish towns, and delivery of 15,000 ducats in three years, to be raised from various products.

Las Casas may or may not have realized that unruly Spaniards on the nearby island of Cubagua would cause trouble. Even before he left Spain with seventy hastily assembled colonists, the Cubagua Spaniards had raided his territory and enslaved some of the inhabitants. When Las Casas reached Puerto Rico in January 1521, he learned that the Indians, in revenge, had killed two Dominicans and destroyed the Dominican monastery at Chiribichi, Venezuela. A punitive expedition of Spaniards had already sailed from Hispaniola to take more slaves.

Las Casas tried but failed to stop this expedition, under Gonzalo de Ocampo, when it touched at Puerto Rico. He then anxiously lodged his colonists in Puerto Rico and went to Santo Domingo to protest to the Spanish authorities. They put him off while the first slaves began to arrive from Venezuela. At last, in desperation, Las Casas agreed to merge his expedition with Ocampo's, to share the profits with the governing officials, and to permit the Spaniards to enslave Indians he judged guilty of cannibalism (presumably, he planned to find none guilty).

The result was a complete disaster. The colonists Las Casas had left in Puerto Rico ran off with Ponce de León to try to conquer Florida. When Las Casas reached his territory at Cumaná, in August 1521, he had only a small staff and a royal official. The Franciscans there welcomed him warmly, but Ocampo's soldiers departed for Hispaniola or Cubagua. From Cubagua, they continued their incursions among Las Casas' future catechumens until the Franciscans persuaded Las Casas to return to Hispaniola to demand protection.

As soon as Las Casas left, his second-in-command, Francisco de Soto, sailed off in the community's one remaining ship—to hunt slaves. A few days later, on January 10, 1522, the Indians rose and killed a lay brother, a gunner, an Indian interpreter, and the returning de Soto, and then burned the Franciscan monastery.

Las Casas' ship went astray and landed him at the wrong end

of Hispaniola, prolonging his journey by weeks. As he plodded over the hills toward Santo Domingo, passers-by told him the news of the massacre, which had already reached the capital: "The Indians of the Pearl Coast have slain the cleric Bartolomé de Las Casas and all his household!"[14]

Las Casas was stunned. He "thought it was a divine judgment, punishing and afflicting him"[15] for compromising his principles when he made the agreement with the Spanish authorities. His hopes for a Spanish-Indian utopia shattered, his confidence that he was divinely chosen to defend the Indians shaken, he turned his back on this world. At the urging of Fray Domingo de Betanzos, he entered the Dominican novitiate in Santo Domingo and was professed a Dominican one year later, in December 1523. For eleven years, in his own words, "he, to all appearances, slept"[16] — while the tide of Spanish conquest swept on, over Mexico and Peru.

During this interval, we have only glimpses of his activities. After the required four-year course in Scripture, Patristics, and Thomas Aquinas, he was sent in 1527 to found the Dominican monastery at Puerto de Plata, on the north coast of Hispaniola. Here, as prior, he refused to grant absolution to Spanish colonists unless they would make restitution for goods and services taken from the Indians. Here, also, he began the *History of the Indies*, perhaps because he learned that the former encomendero Oviedo had written a general history of the Indies which would inevitably favor the conquistadors. In January 1534, he went out into the wilderness and pacified a romantic Indian rebel, Enriquillo, who had successfully defied the secular authorities of Hispaniola.

In June 1534, Las Casas left Hispaniola to accompany the newly-appointed bishop of Peru, Tomás de Berlanga, to his post. They reached Panama safely, but when Las Casas set out ahead for Peru dangerous calms forced his ship back to Nicaragua. Here he once more became active as "Protector of the Indians." (Las Casas had been given this state office in 1516 but how long he formally occupied it is unknown.) Finding that Governor Rodrigo de Contreras planned an expedition of conquest and slave-hunting, he attacked it so violently that many of Contreras' soldiers refused to serve on it. Then he wrote the Empress Doña

Isabella and got the expedition postponed for two years.

He journeyed to Guatemala, and was there on June 9, 1537, when Pope Paul III issued the crucial bull *Sublimis Deus*. *Sublimis Deus*, reflecting the ideas of the Dominicans, proclaimed the rationality of the Indians and their capacity to receive the Faith. They were not "beasts who talked,"[17] as the conquistadors called them.

Sublimis Deus became a cornerstone of Las Casas' applied theology. He now wrote, in Latin, *The Only Method of Attracting All People to the True Faith*, in which he refuted the argument that armed conquest was a necessary preliminary to conversion. Citing the teachings of the Church Fathers and the example of Christ, Las Casas demonstrated the inexpediency and injustice of all wars against the Indians and pleaded for conversion only by appeals to the reason and the will. "War also fills every place with highwaymen, thieves, ravishers, fires, and murders," wrote Las Casas. "Indeed, what is war but general murder and robbery among many?"[18] [Las Casas actually wrote the first version of *The Only Way* in 1534; it ws carried to Rome in 1536 and was the direct inspiration and basis of the encyclical *Sublimis Deus*. See Bibliography below: Parish, ed., *The Only Way*; Parish, "Las Casas' Spirituality"; Parish with Weidman, *Las Casas en México*, v. 1, all 1991. —Eds.]

In 1537, with the Dominicans Fray Pedro de Angulo, Fray Luis Cáncer, and Fray Rodrigo de Ladrada, Las Casas organized a mission to convert the fierce natives of Tuzulutlán, called the Land of War by the Spaniards, in northeast Guatemala. This time, Las Casas did not offer to raise money for the king, as he had in the ill-fated Venezuela project. His agreement with Governor Alonso de Maldonado provided simply that no encomiendas be granted in Tuzulutlán and that no Spaniards be permitted to enter the territory for five years. One of the famous episodes of mission history followed.

According to the traditional account, the friars composed *canciones*, songs in the Quiché language of the natives, which told about the creation of the world, man's fall, the life of Christ, and the last judgment. Then they found four Christian Indian merchants to whom they taught the songs. The Indian merchants journeyed to the Land of War and so enchanted the inhabitants with their ballads and their stories about the good friars—white men without weapons, who sought neither gold nor women— that the natives invited the Dominicans to visit them. A leading cacique was converted and baptized Juan. Juan built a church, and the Faith spread rapidly, other important caciques being baptized Jorge, Miguel, and Gaspar. All were made "dons" by the emperor, and soon the Land of War was renamed Verapaz— True Peace. It now appears, however, that this traditional account is somewhat fictionalized—that the work of Las Casas and his fellow Dominicans was slow, prudent, quiet, with more accomplished after 1538 than before.

In 1539, the Dominicans dispatched Las Casas to bring missionaries from the homeland. Accompanied by Fray Rodrigo de Ladrada, who was to become his lifelong companion, he returned to Spain in June 1540. He recruited Dominicans for his mission and obtained capitulations from the Council of the Indies confirming his contract to Christianize Tuzulutlán. He also won support for his view that Indians should not be baptized en masse, without instruction, as was done by Fray Toribio de Benavente ("Motolinía"). Most important, he secured Charles V's permission to remain in Spain until Charles came back from waging war against France to hear Las Casas' proposals. Thus the "Protector of the Indians" returned to court at a time when, thanks to widespread complaints about mistreatment of the Indians, the climate of opinion was favorable to his ideas.

Heartened by the emperor's interest, Las Casas plunged into the struggle for reform. He wrote the first version of the *Very Brief Account of the Destruction of the Indies* and read it at court, to shock his hearers with lurid details of Spanish cruelty—with memorable anecdotes like that about the cacique Hatuey, who chose not to go to a heaven occupied by Christians but "rather to hell so as not to be where Spaniards were."[19] He charged members of the Council of the Indies with corruption, and he argued in favor of specific reforms, especially the immediate abolition of the encomienda system and the placing of all Indians under the Crown.

Charles V did not want a neofeudalism, based on the encomienda, to develop in the New World. Because of this consideration, along with pressure from Las Casas and others, the emperor promulgated the New Laws on November 20, 1542. These gave Las Casas almost everything he asked for: no more Indians were to be enslaved, officials were to be deprived of their encomiendas, and other encomiendas were to be transferred to the Crown upon the deaths of their holders. In addition, Charles V dismissed certain council members, and demoted the president, Cardinal García de Loaysa. Las Casas had triumphed.

Or so it seemed. The problem of enforcement remained, and Las Casas found himself in the thick of that battle. Court officials were eager to have him removed from Spain. The powerful secretary, Francisco de los Cobos, offered him the rich bishopric of Cuzco, in Peru, but he refused it. However, when he was then offered the impoverished bishopric of Chiapa, in southern Mexico next to Verapaz, he felt he had to accept. With a large continent of Dominican missionaries, he sailed from San Lúcar on July 10, 1544, for the Indies, where the unpopular laws had to be administered.

Las Casas' career as bishop was short and stormy. When his fleet reached Santo Domingo, the Spaniards there turned their backs on "one of the most hated men who had ever been in the Indies"[20] and refused him provisions. After completing his arduous journey—losing nine friars by shipwreck and having to navigate his own ship because of the incompetence of the pilot—he was received in mountainous Chiapa by sixty suspicious Spanish colonists. As soon as he announced that he would refuse absolution to Spaniards who did not free their Indian slaves or make restitution of wealth gained from encomiendas, the suspicion turned to hatred and harassment. There were obscene songs about him and threats against his life. His dean, Gil Quintana, scandalously defied him and gave absolution to slaveholders.

The beleaguered Las Casas sought solace by a tour of the churches of Tuzulutlán, where the Indians welcomed him with floral arches and tears of joy. But when he journeyed to the Audiencia de los Confines, in Gracias á Dios, to seek support against the rebels of Chiapa, the Audiencia gave him scant satisfaction. Its president was Alonso de Maldonado, who had approved the Tuzulutlán mission but was now hostile because of his marriage to the daughter of a wealthy encomendero. Maldonado began each session by denouncing "that lunatic"[21] Bishop Las Casas. (Months later, Las Casas secured Maldonado's transfer.)

When Las Casas returned to Chiapa, the resentful citizens tried to block his entry. He slipped in and confronted them in his cathedral, where they petitioned to be allowed to keep their property, that is, their Indians; they wanted more confessors like Dean Quintana. Upon Las Casas' refusing, there was a riot, followed by an uneasy truce.

Meanwhile, in Mexico, Inspector Francisco Tello de Sandoval had suspended the Law of Inheritance indefinitely because of the turbulent opposition it had encountered. Peru was in flames from a Spanish revolt against the changes instigated by the New Laws, as was Nicaragua. Las Casas therefore decided to go back to Spain and try to save his reforms. Then news came, perhaps before he could start, that on October 20, 1545, the emperor had revoked the key Law of Inheritance, which had provided for phasing out the encomiendas.

Las Casas, nevertheless, departed for Spain, traveling first to Mexico City in June 1546, for a conference of bishops. The capital braced itself against his coming—but with the New Laws partially rescinded, passions had subsided. People in the streets merely stared at the seventy-two-year-old Las Casas; a few even said, "There goes the holy bishop, the true father of the Indians!"[22] While here, Las Casas composed his *Confesionario*, or rules for confessors, to be applied in his own diocese by Canon Juan de Pereira, whom he left in charge.

When the contents of the *Confesionario* leaked out to the public, they created a scandal and caused Las Casas to be accused of treason. He had insisted on every penitent's freeing his Indian slaves and making full restitution before receiving absolution, no matter what heirs were waiting for his property— because the penitent's wealth had been unjustly acquired. But if everything done by Spaniards in the New World had been unlawful, what just claim did Spain have to the Indies? What right did Spaniards have to be there at all? The government confiscated copies of the *Confesionario*, and in 1548 Las Casas was called up before the Council of the Indies to explain his ideas.

Suddenly, Las Casas found himself on the defensive. Not only did he have to spell out his theory of Spain's title to the Indies, which was that Pope Alexander VI had granted Spain the right to evangelize but not to conquer; he also now encountered, for the first time, a formidable literary champion of the conquistadors' point of view, Juan Ginés de Sepúlveda, the emperor's chronicler and Renaissance humanist. In 1548, Las Casas had prevented the Spanish publication of Sepúlveda's *Democrates Alter*, which defended wars of conquest. In retaliation, Sepúlveda had played a part in the government's confiscation of copies of Las Casas' *Confesionario*.

Las Casas tried to stem the reaction by redoubling his protests against Spanish exploitation of the Indians. Finally, in 1550, Charles V became so troubled by Las Casas' criticisms that he ordered all conquests in the New World halted! A commission of theologians and jurists was instructed to hear Sepúlveda and Las Casas debate the justice of the Conquest and to decide on the most lawful method of carrying out the Spanish occupation of America.

The "great debate" took place between July and September 1550 in Valladolid. There were no Lincoln-Douglas fireworks — the antagonists did not confront each other — but Las Casas tested the commission's powers of endurance by reading them his long *Defense*, written especially for the occasion, for seven sessions. The polished Sepúlveda summarized his *Democrates Alter* in a few hours. Sepúlveda argued that the Indians' vices justified war against them and also that they were an inferior race needing Spanish tutelage — "slaves by nature," in the words of Aristotle's *Politics*, which Sepúlveda had just translated.[23] Las Casas replied by defending the Indians' rationality and liberty; he even attempted to find reasons for their practice of human sacrifice. In April 1551, the commission met again, but only Sepúlveda appeared before it.

No formal decision was handed down, but according to Giménez Fernández, the majority favored Las Casas. Later policy of the Council of the Indies confirmed this, says Giménez Fernández. Charles V never had revoked the New Laws abolishing slavery and taking encomiendas away from Crown officials; now conquests of the old type were also proscribed.

Las Casas may not have been particularly elated. But there was still much work to be done before retribution was enacted, work best done in Spain, where the fate of millions of Americans was decided. So he resigned his bishopric in August 1550, and in July 1551 contracted for a lifetime lodging for himself and the faithful Ladrada, in the Dominican monastery of San Gregorio, in Valladolid. He now became the permanent, universally recognized "Protector of the Indians" at court.

As a manifesto of his views and a guide for his followers in the New World, Las Casas published eight treatises in Seville, in 1552. (He was there to bid Godspeed to a band of Dominicans leaving for the Americas, and at the same time to study books and documents about Christopher Columbus in the Dominican monastery.) The eight treatises included the controversial *Confesionario*, two treatises on Spain's title to the Indies, an attack on Indian slavery, an attack on the encomienda system, a summary of the Sepúlveda debate, and the sensational *Very Brief Account of the Destruction of the Indies*. The *Very Brief Account* was later translated into six European languages and given wide circulation by the enemies of Spain. It infuriated the conquistadors and helped spread the "Black Legend" (*Leyenda Negra*) of Spanish cruelty.

Between 1554 and 1560, Las Casas fought his last major battle and won it. The conquistadors of Peru offered the nearly bankrupt Philip II, who was in England, between 7 and 9 million ducats to have their encomiendas made perpetual. Las Casas immediately dispatched a fiery letter of protest to the king's confessor, Master Carranza de Miranda, in August 1555 and secured a postponement of Philip's decision. Then he rallied the Indian caciques of Peru; they gave him their power of attorney, in 1559, and, in return for certain rights, offered to top any bid of the conquistadors by 100,000 ducats. More postponements followed, and the scheme was finally dropped because of the corruption of those who had been sent to Peru to implement it. (Of the Spaniards in the Indies, Las Casas wrote, "the best thing imaginable would be to cast them all out, except a few chosen ones.")[24]

For thirteen years, when he was in his seventies and early eighties and his enemies might have hoped for a graceful retirement, Las Casas traveled with the court, clamoring for justice for his clients and most often obtaining it. He was Old Testament prophet and canon lawyer combined, says Father Stafford Poole.[25] Petitions poured into his cell in Valladolid. Friars, priests, and laymen wrote, and he answered with letters of encouragement to his disciples in Spain and the Americas. He was given power of attorney to act for the Indians of Chimalhuacán (1554), Mexico (1556), Lima (1559, 1566), and Rio Hacha (1565). He journeyed from Valladolid (1554) to Toledo (1560) to Madrid (1564). At the same time, he carried on his extensive recruiting of missionaries for the New World.

Somehow, Las Casas also found time to complete his two chief literary works, the *Apologetic History* and the *History of the Indies*. The *Apologetic History*, finished around 1559, had at first been part of the *History of the Indies*. It is a pioneer study in anthropology, containing detailed descriptions of the Indians' lands, social and political organization, religion, customs, etc. Using Aristotelian standards, Las Casas compares the Indians' culture to that of Christian nations and finds it not inferior.

The *History of the Indies*, given a final revision between 1562 and 1564, is Las Casas' fascinating narrative of the discovery and early history of the Americas, 1492-1520. It is particularly rich in material about Columbus. Although it was not to be published for over 300 years, the *History of the Indies* became a mine for later historians like Antonio de Herrera, and was recognized as a classic, while still in manuscript. Both works demonstrate that no one in Europe in the sixteenth century could rival Las Casas in knowledge and experience of the New World.

The "Protector of the Indians" was active until the very end. He had a petition concerning Indian rights presented to the Council of the Indies by a colleague just a few days before his death. Less than three weeks before that, he had kept certain Indians of his beloved Tuzulutlán from being given in encomienda to Juan Rodríguez Cabrillo. In his will, dated March 17, 1564, he described his vocation and told how (like the epic hero Beowulf) he had labored for fifty years for his people, that is, the Indians:

In His goodness and mercy, God considered it right to
choose me as his minister, though unworthy, to plead for
all those peoples of the Indies, possessors of those kingdoms and lands, against wrongs and injuries never before
heard of or seen, received from our Spaniards . . . and to
restore them to the primitive liberty of which they were
unjustly deprived. . . . And I have labored in the court of
the kings of Castile going and coming many times from the
Indies to Castile and from Castile to the Indies, for about
fifty years, since the year 1514, for God alone and from
compassion at seeing perish such multitudes of rational
men, domestic, humble, most mild and simple beings, well
fitted to receive our holy Catholic faith . . . and to be
endowed with all good customs.[26]

His last hours came on July 18, 1566, in the monastery of
Atocha in Madrid. With candle in hand, he begged his Dominican brothers to continue to protect the Indians. He expressed
sorrow for having done so little for them himself, and said he
considered that all he had done had been just. But Las Casas'
"little" was a profound understatement. More accurate had
been an opponent's warning cry fifty years before: "He is a candle that will set everything on fire!"[27]

Today, 400 years after his death, Bartolomé de Las Casas
remains one of the exciting and controversial figures of history.
A hero-saint in Latin America, where statues and pictures of
him abound, he is the subject of vigorous disputes among scholars. The extensive and rapidly growing bibliography of books
and articles about him contains many titles that are not favorable — the conquistadors have their spokesmen still, who question Las Casas' accuracy and accuse him of fanaticism verging
on paranoia. But the majority view, at least in the Western Hem-
isphere, is that which pays tribute to Las Casas as the representative *par excellence* of a New World ideal of liberty and justice
for all men. "When Las Casas spoke at Valladolid for the American Indians," writes Lewis Hanke, "one more painful and fal-
tering step was . . . taken along the road of justice for all races."[28]
Henry R. Wagner considers Las Casas, with his "dream of a free
America,"[29] a greater man than the celebrated Emperor Charles

V. And the Mexican novelist Agustín Yáñez names him the "Father and Doctor of Americanism,"[30] whose "style is, in good part, the style of the continent."[31]

A NOTE ON THE SELECTIONS

The works in Spanish alone by Bartolomé de Las Casas occupy five volumes (double column) of the Biblioteca de Autores Españoles. From these hundreds of pages, and from two other recent publications, the following twenty-eight selections have been chosen. Twenty-six are here translated into English by the editor for the first time. The selections consist of episodes and descriptions from Las Casas' histories, and of expositions or protests concerning Spain's role in the Indies from his other writings. Passages have been chosen because of their eloquence ("Reception in Barcelona"), their depiction of an outstanding historical event ("San Salvador"), their emphasis on an important aspect of Las Casas' thought ("The Restoration of the Indies," "A Defense of Human Sacrifice"), or their weight as historical evidence ("The Conquest of Cuba"). An attempt is made to give the reader an overall view of the contents of the *History of the Indies* and the *Apologetic History*.

The selections are arranged under four categories, including three usually adopted by Las Casas scholars—history, anthropology, and political thought—and a fourth, autobiography, suggested by Professor Raymond Marcus of the University of Paris. Selections under "Historian" illustrate the chief subjects of Las Casas' *History of the Indies*: the enterprise of Columbus, other Spanish expeditions, and the sufferings of the Indians at the hands of the Spaniards, about which Las Casas writes with passionate conviction. Selections under "Autobiographer" reveal the origin of that conviction and show Las Casas in action as Protector of the Indians and would-be colonizer. Selections under "Anthropologist" describe western lands, peoples, crafts, etc., and also illustrate the comparative method employed by Las Casas in his *Apologetic History*—measuring the culture of the New World against that of the Old World by Aristotelian standards. Selections under "Political Thinker" represent Las Casas' most important treatises besides the two histories, and give his arguments for the abolition of the encomienda, the conversion of pagans by peaceful means, and the rationality of the American Indian.

It is the editor's hope that the selections will acquaint the reader with the basic ideas of Bartolomé de Las Casas, as well as with his personality, manifold activities, and literary achievements. It is the editor's further hope that the reader will lay the volume down with the conviction that "here is one of the great men of the Conquest" — that "no matter what may be one's individual reaction to him, Las Casas is a towering figure of his time whose relevance to today's problems is obvious."[32]

NOTES

1. Samuel Eliot Morison, *Admiral of the Ocean Sea* (Boston: Little, Brown, 1942), p. 51.

2. Bartolomé de Las Casas, *Obras Escogidas,* ed. Juan Pérez de Tudela (Madrid: Biblioteca de Autores Españoles, 1957-1958), I, 327.

3. Christopher Columbus, *Journals and Other Documents*, tr. and ed. Samuel Eliot Morison (New York: Heritage Press, 1963), p. 65.

4. Gonzalo Fernández de Oviedo y Valdés, *Historia general y natural de las Indias*, ed. Juan Pérez de Tudela (Madrid: Biblioteca de Autores Españoles, 1959), II, 199.

5. Juan Pérez de Tudela, "Estudio Crítico Preliminar," in Bartolomé de Las Casas, *Obras Escogidas*, ed. Pérez de Tudela (Madrid: Biblioteca de Autores Españoles, 1957-1958), I, xxix. In general, I follow Pérez de Tudela and also Manuel Giménez Fernández, *Breve biografía de Fray Bartolomé de Las Casas* (Seville: Universidad de Sevilla, 1966) in this Introduction.

6. Las Casas, *Obras Escogidas*, II, 421.

7. Henry Raup Wagner and Helen Rand Parish, *The Life and Writings of Bartolomé de las Casas* (Albuquerque: University of New Mexico Press, 1967), p. 16.

8. Las Casas, *Obras Escogidas*, II, 136.

9. Ibid., II, 244.

10. Wagner and Parish, *The Life and Writings of Bartolomé de las Casas*, p. 7.

11. Las Casas, *Obras Escogidas*, II, 357.

12. Las Casas, *Obras Escogidas*, II, 369.

13. Ibid., II, 487. (In his text Sanderlin said here: "Las Casas suggested importing Negro slaves to do the heavy work, but later bitterly regretted making the proposal, when he 'found out . . . that the Negros' captivity was as unjust as the Indians' " [*Obras Escogidas*, II, 487]. This is an old slander based on a misunderstanding of what was in Las Casas' suggestion and ignorance of what really happened. See the footnote on page xix and the introductory note on page 85; see also Pérez, *Bartolomé de las Casas contra Los Negros? Revisión de una leyenda.* — Ed.)

14. Ibid., II, 563.

15. Ibid.

16. Ibid., II, 567.

17. Pérez de Tudela, "Estudio Crítico Preliminar," p. xxxi.

18. Bartolomé de Las Casas, *Del Único Modo de Atraer a Todos los Pueblos a la Verdadera Religión*, ed. Augustín Millares Carlo (Mexico City: Fondo de Cultura Económica, 1942), p. 399.

19. Las Casas, *Obras Escogidas*, V, 142.

20. Antonio de Remesal, *Historia general de las Indias occidentales* (Madrid, 1619), II, 108, as quoted in Wagner and Parish, *The Life and Writings of Bartolomé de las Casas*, p. 135.

21. Ibid., II, 59, as quoted in Wagner and Parish, *The Life and Writings of Bartolomé de las Casas*, p. 148.

22. Ibid., II, 108-109, as quoted in Wagner and Parish, *The Life and Writings of Bartolomé de las Casas*, p. 159.

23. Lewis Hanke, *The Spanish Struggle for Justice in the Conquest of America* (Boston: Little, Brown, 1965), p. 114.

24. Las Casas, *Obras Escogidas*, V, 447.

25. Stafford Poole, C. M., "Introduction" to Bartolomé de Las Casas, *Defense Against the Persecutors and Slanderers of the Peoples of the New World Discovered Across the Ocean*, ed. Ernest J. Burrus, S. J. (Madrid: Series José Porrua Turanza, Editorial José Venero, 1971).

26. Las Casas, *Obras Escogidas*, V, 539.

27. Letter from the Jeronymites to Cardinal Cisneros, as quoted in Pérez de Tudela, "Estudio Crítico Preliminar," p. lxix.

28. Hanke, *The Spanish Struggle for Justice in the Conquest of America*, p. 132.

29. Wagner and Parish, *The Life and Writings of Bartolomé de las Casas*, p. 250.

30. Agustín Yáñez, "Prólogo" in Bartolomé de Las Casas, *Doctrina*, ed. Yáñez (Mexico City: Universidad Nacional Autónoma, 1951), p. ix.

31. Agustín Yáñez, *Fray Bartolomé de Las Casas* (3rd edition; Mexico City: Editorial Xochitl, 1966), p. 190.

32. Lewis Hanke, letter to the editor, October 9, 1969.

PART I

HISTORIAN

THE HISTORY OF THE INDIES

When Las Casas sought a grant of land in Venezuela in 1519, one of his most determined opponents was the royal official Gonzalo Fernández de Oviedo, who ridiculed his project of peaceful conversion of the Indians. Seven years later, in 1526, Oviedo published a treatise on the plants and animals of the New World containing a statement that would alarm Las Casas — an announcement that Oviedo had written a general history of the Indies.

Since such a history would be highly unfavorable in its discussion of the Indians, the prospect of its appearance may have stimulated Las Casas to undertake his own *History of the Indies*. At any rate, he did begin his masterpiece the very next year, 1527, in the Dominican monastery in Puerto de Plata, Hispaniola. His purpose, he said later, was not to seek literary fame, nor to entertain and flatter princes — perhaps a hint that Oviedo had the latter motive — but solely to meet "the need for real knowledge and the light of truth among all ranks concerning this Indian world."[1] Thus Las Casas' *History of the Indies*, like the medieval chronicles in which he was deeply read, was to have a teaching function. It would show rulers the paths of righteousness; it was "for the well-being and benefit of all Spain."[2]

He worked on it in Hispaniola until 1534. Then he emerged from monastic retirement to take up once more the battle for the Indians — to make history instead of writing it. For twenty years he found himself "unable to finish this history because of my great travels and occupations."[3] Lewis Hanke has plausibly conjectured that Las Casas' review of the records of injustice to the Indians in order to obtain documentation for his book may have inspired him to reenter the combat.[4]

In August 1550, Las Casas resigned his bishopric, and in July

1551, he contracted for lifetime residence in the Dominican monastery of San Gregorio, in Valladolid. While he continued to serve as "Protector of the Indians," he was able to resume work on his manuscript, which had accompanied him back and forth across the Atlantic. He now detached the descriptive material about Indian religion, economy, government, and so forth and expanded it into his encyclopedic *Apologetic History*. At the same time, he carried his *History of the Indies* down to 1520. This was just half of the period he had planned to cover (1492-1550), but he died before he could complete the work. Two sixteenth-century manuscripts of the *History of the Indies* are extant: Las Casas' autograph, and a clear copy made for him, with marginal additions in his hand.

Although Oviedo's general history, with its attacks on the Indians, had been published in 1555, Las Casas requested that his *History of the Indies* not be printed until forty years after his death. Perhaps he hoped for a more objective reception then, when the passions inflamed by his *Very Brief Account of the Destruction of the Indies* (1552) might have subsided. Actually, owing to Spain's growing sensitivity to criticism of its colonial empire, Las Casas' *History of the Indies* was not published until 1875.

The two major themes of the *History of the Indies* are Columbus' discovery of America and the tragic fate of the Indians. Book I (1492-1500) begins with a statement of God's plan for the conversion of the races and of Columbus' appointed role as the one who would "first open the gates of this Ocean Sea"[5] for the passage of the faith of Christ to the Indies. It describes the Portuguese-Spanish expansion to the islands of the eastern Atlantic as a preliminary to Columbus' accomplishment; narrates in detail his first three voyages; and includes accounts of other important events in the Indies, such as Roldán's rebellion against Bartholomew Columbus and Hojeda's voyage of 1499 to Guinea and Venezuela.

Book II (1511-1520) describes Nicolás de Ovando's institutionalizing of the encomienda system in Hispaniola; Columbus' fourth voyage and death; the depopulation of the Bahamas; the conquest of Puerto Rico and the first reconnaissance of Cuba; the expansion along the northern coast of South America to

Panama; and the coming of the Dominicans to Hispaniola.

Book III (1511-1520) covers the conquest of Cuba; Balboa's trek to the South Sea; the tyrannical rule of Pedrarias Dávila in the Isthmus; the discovery of Yucatán; Cortés' landing in Mexico; and Las Casas' conversion and early efforts in behalf of the natives, climaxed by the failure of his colony in Venezuela.

Las Casas is criticized for his many digressions, such as his discourse on the source of the Nile and his four chapters on the location of the earthly paradise, both interrupting his account of Columbus' third voyage. However, Las Casas clearly marks these digressions at beginning and end (for example, "Having finished this digression, let us return to our history"[6]), and he occasionally includes important contemporary material in them, as in his discussion of the claim that Amerigo Vespucci was the discoverer of South America. He frequently gives a brief recapitulation of the previous chapter, or chapters, at the start of a new one, to orient the reader.

His sentences are usually long and involved, full of references to Greek and Latin authors; yet he can write quite simply and directly, as when he describes a killing at Caonao (see pp. 52-53) or relates a clash with Bishop Fonseca (see pp. 82-83). His participation in a number of scenes and his sharp impressions of the actors—Cortés the opportunist, Pedrarias Dávila the tyrant, the haughty Fonseca—give immediacy and life to his *History*.

His statistics are unreliable. For instance, he first estimated the native population of Hispaniola at 1 million (as did Oviedo), then at 3 million, whereas scholars today have placed it as low as 100,000. But many of Las Casas' contemporaries are guilty of similar exaggerations. Otherwise, modern researchers confirm the essential truth of his narrative. He is almost alone among sixteenth-century historians in scrupulously citing printed sources. He expresses skepticism about hearsay stories, admits when his memory is uncertain, and quotes extensively from his collection of documents, by far the largest owned by any writer of that period.

Lewis Hanke thinks that Las Casas possessed the cardinal virtues of a great historian, including "a sense of the sweep of history."[7] Like his contemporaries, Las Casas considered the

discovery of the New World the eighth wonder of all time—
perhaps the most important event since the coming of Christ.
Although he disclaimed literary ambition, he wished for the
"pen of Tullius Cicero, with its eloquence,"[8] in order to celebrate the magnitude of Columbus' achievement. In spite of its
lack of literary elegance—perhaps in part because of its passion
as well as its wealth of detail—Las Casas' *History of the Indies*
stands as the epic of the discovery of America.

NOTES

1. Bartolomé de Las Casas, *Obras Escogidas*, ed. Juan Pérez de
Tudela (Madrid: Biblioteca de Autores Españoles, 1957-1958), I, 10.
2. Ibid., I, 15.
3. Ibid., I, 16.
4. Lewis Hanke, *Bartolomé de Las Casas: Historian* (Gainesville:
University of Florida Press, 1952), p. 17.
5. Las Casas, *Obras Escogidas*, I, 21.
6. Ibid., I, 390.
7. Hanke, *Bartolomé de Las Casas: Historian*, p. 97.
8. Las Casas, *Obras Escogidas*, I, 229.

❈{ 1 }❈

Prologue: *Why He Wrote History*

The following selection, from the lengthy Prologue composed in Spain in 1552, gives Las Casas' reasons for writing the History of the Indies (Obras Escogidas, *I, 15-16.*)*

I wished to accept this responsibility and, among my many other concerns, to undertake this work, not a small one, first and foremost for the honor and glory of God, and the manifesting of his profound and unsearchable judgments. . . . Second, for the common benefit, spiritual and temporal, which can come to all these infinite Indian peoples, if perchance they are not finished off first, before this history is completed. Third, not to give relish, nor to please or flatter kings, but to defend the honor and royal renown of the illustrious sovereigns of Castile, because those persons who will know of the irreparable damage done in these vast regions . . . will not know what the Catholic kings, past and present, always ordered provided, and did themselves provide, and the end they aimed at. . . .

Fourth, for the well-being and benefit of all Spain, because when it is known in what consists the good or evil of these Indies,

From Bartolomé de Las Casas, *Obras Escogidas*, 5 vols., ed. Juan Pérez de Tudela (Madrid: Biblioteca de Autores Españoles, 1957-1958). All the selections in Part I—Historian are taken from the *History of the Indies*.

*Page references to the source of each of the passages are given to assist the reader who wishes to consult the original Spanish.

I believe that it will be known in what consists the good and evil
of Spain. Fifth, to give readers clarity and certainty about many
ancient things concerning the beginnings of the discoveries. . . .
Sixth, to free my Spanish race from error, from the serious,
pernicious illusion in which it lives and has always lived until
today, judging that these oceanic peoples lack the nature of men,
considering them brute beasts, incapable of virtue and learning,
corrupting the good they possess and exaggerating the evil
among them. . . .

Seventh, to moderate the boasting and vainglory of many, and
to reveal the injustice of not a few, who pride themselves on
vicious and execrable wickedness . . . so that, for the benefit of
posterity, evil may be known and distinguished from good, likewise great sins and vices from virtues. And no one should marvel
that I rebuke and detest the misdeeds of the Spaniards, nor
should it be attributed to unkindness or folly, according to what
Polybius says in his *History of the Romans*, Book I: "He who
chooses the office of historian should sometimes exalt enemies
with high praise, if their excellent deeds deserve it, and at other
times should severely upbraid and rebuke friends when their
mistakes are worthy of blame." . . .

Eighth and last, to show by a different road than others have
taken, how numerous and how great were the marvelous deeds
in these Indies, actions never accomplished, we believe, in the
centuries now forgotten. All, however, is directed to this end:
that through knowledge of virtuous works . . . posterity may be
heartened to imitate these works; and also that through tidings
of culpable acts, divine punishments, and the wretched end of
their perpetrators, men may fear to do evil. For as Diodorus
said [in the Proem to his *History*], it is a beautiful thing to learn
from mistakes made by those who lived in the past, how we
should order our lives, as many have ordered theirs.

❧{ 2 }❧

A Portrait of Columbus

The following selection, from Book I, Chapter 2, gives Las Casas' impression of Christopher Columbus, whom he observed on various occasions. Las Casas apparently did not know Columbus personally, but he was well acquainted with Columbus' two sons and two brothers. (Obras Escogidas, I, 20-22.)

The time of God's merciful wonders having now arrived, when in these parts of the earth (the seed or word of life once sown) there was to be gathered the abundant harvest of the predestined ... , the Divine Master chose, among the sons of Adam ... , that great and illustrious Columbus ... to be entrusted with one of the eminent achievements which He sought to bring about in the present century. ...

This chosen man was of the Genoese race, of a certain place in the province of Genoa. What place it might be where he was born or what name such a place had is not clear, except from what he was usually called before he arrived at the rank he later attained, that is, Christopher Columbus of Terra-rubia. ...

He was called, then, Christopher, that is, *Christum ferens*, which means bearer of Christ, and thus he sometimes signed himself. And in truth he was the first who opened the gates of this Ocean Sea, through which he entered and introduced himself to these most remote lands, and to kingdoms until then so hidden from our Savior Jesus Christ and His blessed name—he who before any other was worthy to give tidings of Christ and to bring these countless races, forgotten for so many centuries, to worship Him.

His surname was Columbus, which means new settler. This surname suited him in that by his industry and labors he was the cause ... of an infinite number of souls ... having gone and going every day of late to colonize that triumphant city of Heaven. Also it suited him because he first carried people from Spain ... to plant colonies, which consist of new inhabitants brought from outside. Settled among the natives of these vast lands, they would constitute a strong new Christian church and happy republic, illustrious and widespread.

In what concerned his outer person and the condition of his body, he was taller than average; his face long, and having an air of authority; his nose aquiline; his eyes blue; his complexion light and tending toward bright red; his beard and hair red when he was young, although they soon turned gray from his labors. He was gracious and cheerful, a good speaker, and, as mentioned in the Portuguese history [Juan de Barros, *Asia*, Book III, Chapter 2], eloquent and boastful in his business affairs. He was serious but not too serious, affable with strangers, kindly and pleasant with those of his own household ... and thus he was able to stir affection for himself easily in those who saw him.

In short, in his bearing and countenance he presented the image of a person of high rank and authority, one worthy of all reverence. He was sober and temperate in eating and drinking, in clothing and footwear. It was commonly said that he spoke cheerfully in familiar conversation, or indignantly when he rebuked anyone or became angry with him: "I give you to God — don't you like this or that?" or "Why did you do this or that?"

In matters of the Christian religion, without doubt he was a Catholic, and very devout. In almost everything he did or said or wished to begin, he always interposed: "In the name of the Holy Trinity I will do this, or this will come," or "I hope this will be." In any letter or other thing that he wrote, he placed at the head *Jesus cum Maria sit nobis in via* ["Jesus and Mary be with us on the way"] — and I now have in my possession many of these writings, in his own hand. His oath was sometimes, "I swear by San Fernando." When he wished to affirm something of great importance in his letters, especially when writing to the sovereigns, he would say, "I swear that this is the truth."

He kept the fasts of the Church most faithfully. He confessed and received communion often. He read all the canonical offices like a churchman or a religious. He strongly opposed blasphemy and oaths and was very devoted to Our Lady and to the seraphic father, St. Francis. He seemed very grateful to God for benefits received from the divine hand, wherefore, as in the proverb, every hour he confessed that God had given him great rewards, as He had David.

When gold or precious things were brought him, he entered his oratory, knelt, summoned the bystanders, and said, "Let us give thanks to our Lord, who has considered us worthy to discover so many good things." He was very zealous for the divine service; eager and desirous for the conversion of these peoples of the Indies. ... And he was especially affected and devoted to the idea that God should consider him worthy of aiding in some way to regain the Holy Sepulchre.... He begged the most serene queen, Doña Isabella, to make a vow to spend all the riches which came to the sovereigns through his discovery to win the land and the holy house of Jerusalem; and so the Queen did. ...

He was a man of great courage, of high spirits, of lofty thoughts, inclined naturally—from what can be gathered of his life, deeds, writings, and conversation—to undertake worthy feats and outstanding enterprises. He was patient, long-suffering (as will appear further below), a pardoner of injuries, and one who sought nothing, according to what is told of him, but that those who had offended him acknowledge their errors and that the wrongdoers be reconciled with him. He was most constant, and endowed with forbearance in labors and adversities ... which were incredible and infinite, always having great confidence in Divine Providence. And truly, from what I heard from him and my own father, who went with him when he returned to settle this island of Hispaniola in 1493—and from other persons who accompanied him and others who served him —he always had and kept an affectionate faithfulness and devotion toward the sovereigns.

❖{ 3 }❖

The Verdict of Salamanca

The following selection, from Book I, Chapter 29, describes the deliberations of the commission organized in 1486 to investigate Columbus' proposed voyage. Columbus' project was rejected because he greatly underestimated the distance between Europe and Asia—not because the commission thought the earth was flat. The "round earth versus flat earth" debate was a later legend, perpetuated by Washington Irving. (Obras Escogidas, I, 108-112.)

In the preceding chapter [*Historia de las Indias*, Book I, Chapter 28], it was apparent that Christopher Columbus had good and sufficient reason to leave the king of Portugal because of the hypocritical behavior of the king. ... Reflecting now that if the sovereigns of Castile should not accept his proposal, he ought not to have to spend a great part of his life seeking lords who would give him the necessary favor and assistance, he decided that while he went to Castile, a brother of his called Bartholomew Columbus should go to the king of England with the same request—should propose the same enterprise to that king.

This brother was a prudent, vigorous man, shrewder and less naïve, it would appear, than Christopher Columbus. He was a Latinist, very wise in human affairs, and especially learned and experienced in things of the sea. I believe that he was little less skilled than his brother in cosmography and related matters, and in making or painting charts of navigation, spheres, and other instruments of that art, and I presume that in some of these he surpassed him, although perhaps he had learned from him. He was taller than average and had a commanding, honorable bearing, although not so much so as the Admiral. This brother departed for England.

According to Las Casas, Bartholomew Columbus soon returned to Portugal without having reached his destination. He sailed with Bartholomew Dias on Dias' voyage to the Cape of Good Hope, 1587-1588—then left again for England.

In 1484, or at the beginning of 1485, . . . Christopher Columbus left Portugal as furtively as he could, fearing that the king would order him stopped. And no doubt the king would have detained him, for seeing that his cast [a secret westward voyage made by the Portuguese to test Columbus' theory] had gone astray . . . the king was trying to restore the said Christopher Columbus to his favor, either to draw from him better, more certain clues in order to send ships again himself, without Columbus, or because he truly wanted the business disclosed and concluded by Columbus' hand. But in the end, Columbus acted more prudently than the king had at the beginning. Taking his little son Diego, he went with Diego to the town of Palos, where he was perhaps acquainted with one of the mariners, or with some religious of St. Francis, in the monastery named Santa Maria de la Rábida, which is a quarter of a league outside the town, or a little more. Here he left his little son Diego Columbus in the care of the friars.

He then departed for the court, at that season in the city of Córdoba, from whence the Catholic sovereigns were providing for the war in Granada, with which they were much preoccupied. When he arrived at court, January 20, 1485, he entered upon a terrible, unceasing battle, painful and prolonged; perhaps a battle with real weapons would not have been so grim or frightful to him as this one, considering how he gave information to so many who did not understand him, although they presumed to; how he answered and endured many who did not know or esteem him, receiving insulting words which afflicted his spirit. And since the first step in difficult negotiations in the courts of

kings is to give an extensive report of what one intends to achieve
to those most approved of by and nearest to the prince ... he
tried to speak with and inform distinguished persons who were
then at court, and who, he felt, could aid him.

*As persons of influence, Las Casas names Cardinal D. Pedro
González de Mendoza, Fray Diego de Deza, Commander Cár-
denas, Chamberlain Juan Cabrero, and the prior of Prado—
Fray Hernando de Talavera who was the queen's confessor.
Talavera organized the commission which considered Colum-
bus' project during several sessions held at the University of
Salamanca, as described below.*

All these, or some of them, negotiated to bring it about that
Columbus be heard by the sovereigns and make them a report
of what he wished to do and came to offer. ... The sovereigns
heard and understood his request, but superficially, because of
their great preoccupation with the said war (for this is a general
rule, that when kings are at war they neither have nor wish to
have much understanding of other matters). But graciously and
with cheerful countenances they agreed to commit it to learned
persons who would listen to Christopher Columbus more particularly, discover the nature of the transaction and the evidence
he gave for it ... and afterward make a complete report to Their
Highnesses.

They entrusted it chiefly to the said prior of Prado, and
ordered him to summon persons who he thought understood
cosmography well, persons who were not very numerous at that
time in Castile. ... These met many times, and Christopher
Columbus proposed his enterprise, giving reasons and authorities so they would consider it feasible—although he omitted the
most pressing reasons so that what had happened when he was
with the king of Portugal would not occur again.

Some asked how it could be that there had been no news of
these Indies for so many thousands of years ... when there had
been a Ptolemy and many other astrologers, cosmographers, and
sages who would have understood a little, or much, about them
and left it in writing. ... To affirm what Christopher Columbus
affirmed was to seek to know, or guess, more than anyone else.

Others argued in this manner: that the world was infinitely large, and that therefore it would be impossible in many years' navigation to arrive at the end of the East by sailing west, as Christopher Columbus professed. They cited a quotation from Seneca in *De las Suasorias*, Book I, in which he says that many sages formerly doubted whether the Ocean Sea could be navigated, supposing it infinite; and even if it could be navigated, it was very doubtful whether there were lands in the other part; and even if there were lands, whether they were habitable; and if they were habitable, whether it would be possible to go to seek and find them. They did not observe that Seneca says these words by way of argument; and although the sages whom Seneca cites were skeptical about the end of India toward the East, these sages of our times inferred that the same reasoning applied to the navigation which Christopher Columbus offered to make from the end of Spain toward the west.

Others, who showed themselves more learned in mathematics, touched on astrology and cosmography, and said that only a very small portion of this lower sphere of water and earth was exposed; all the rest was covered with water, and therefore it was not possible to navigate except along the shores or coasts, as the Portuguese did past Guinea. These who affirmed this had read very few books and had studied navigation less. They added that whoever sailed due west, as Christopher Columbus professed, could not return afterward. Assuming that the world was round and that going toward the west one went downhill . . . on the return it would be necessary to climb uphill, something which ships could not do. This was an excellent, profound reason, and a sign of having understood the affair well!

Others cited St Augustine, who . . . denied that there were antipodes, that is, those who we say have their feet opposite ours; so they carried on a refrain, "St. Augustine doubts it!" He who brought up the matter of the five zones was not missing. According to many, three of these zones are completely uninhabitable, and two habitable; this was also the general opinion of the ancients, who after all didn't know much. Others brought in other reasons not worth mentioning here. Perhaps there were others who naturally have a spirit of contradiction, so that they find something wrong with everything and do not lack reasons

with which to oppose anything, however useful and intelligible
it may be.

In short, this business was for the time being lost in a great
gabble. And although Christopher Columbus answered them
and gave solutions for their arguments ... for them to understand his reasons he would first have had to take away their
mistaken principles ... something always more difficult than
teaching the chief doctrine itself. It was said to be thus with
Timotheus, a famous flute player who charged anyone double
who came to him for instruction but brought with him rules
taught by another; because, said Timotheus, he would have two
labors with such a one: first, to unteach what had already been
learned, and this was the greater task, and second, to teach him
music and his own method of playing.

For this reason, Christopher Columbus could scarcely satisfy
those lords whom the sovereigns had ordered to assemble. They
considered his promises and offers impossible ... and went with
this opinion to the sovereigns. ... They persuaded the sovereigns
that it was not fitting ... to favor a business so weakly founded
... because the sovereigns would lose the money they spent on
it and would weaken their royal authority, without any profit.

In short, the sovereigns ordered that an answer be given
Christopher Columbus dismissing him for that season, although
not completely depriving him of the hope of their returning to
the matter when Their Highnesses saw themselves more at leisure, which they were not then because of their great concern
with the war in Granada.

❖{ 4 }❖

San Salvador

The following selection, from Book I, Chapters 39 and 40, describes a crucial change Columbus made in his course, a near mutiny of his sailors, and his arrival in the New World on October 11-12, 1492. (Obras Escogidas, I, 137-142.)

Because Our Lord had now decided to hasten the time in which He expected to keep faith with Christopher Columbus and show that He had chosen him for this, and also to liberate him from the great danger he was sustaining from those impatient and incredulous people the crews ... and to console all, on Sunday, October 7, at sunrise, the caravel *Niña* ran up a flag on the masthead and fired a bombard as a signal that there was land ahead. The *Niña* was going in front because she was a faster sailer and also ... to win the grant of an annuity of 10,000 maravedis, which the queen had promised to the one who first sighted land. ...

Christopher Columbus had also commanded that at sunrise and sunset all the ships should unite with him, because these are the two times more suitable than others, when the exhalations or mists of the sea do not prevent one from seeing farther across the ocean or land. Then, in the afternoon, as they did not see the land which those on the *Niña* had announced, and it had been only cloud scenery, ... and as Christopher Columbus saw that a great multitude of birds was passing from the north toward the southwest, which was a clear and certain sign that they were going toward land to sleep or perhaps were fleeing from winter ... he therefore resolved to abandon the western course he had been holding and to turn his prow toward the west southwest ... and sail for two days on that course. He remembered that the Portuguese had discovered the majority of the islands they hold today by ... following birds they saw flying swiftly, chiefly toward afternoon. ...

If he had continued on the western course, and Castilian impatience had not interfered, doubtless he would have reached the mainland of Florida, and afterward New Spain ... and it would have been a miracle if he had ever returned to Castile. But God, Who governs, rules, and knows all, managed the affair much better than he or any other could have desired or asked. ...

Monday, October 8, he navigated toward the west southwest, and then ... a large number of different birds appeared, including crows, ducks, one pelican, and, above all, many small field birds, one of which was caught by the sailors in the ship. All rejoiced at this as if they had seen something great. ... These birds were all going toward the southwest. ...

Their joy increased, because they were having a very smooth sea, like the river at Seville. The air was very mild, like April in Seville, ... the sea weed they were accustomed to see was very fresh, for all which Christopher Columbus gave many thanks to Our Lord. ... Tuesday, October 9, he navigated ... eleven leagues during the day and twenty and one half at night. He counted it seventeen for the sailors. All night they heard birds passing. The next day, Wednesday, October 10, the wind grew stronger and ... they ran fifty-nine leagues. He made it forty-four in the public reckoning.

Then, as the sailors saw how far they were going and that the signs both of the small birds and of the large numbers of birds came to naught, ... all of them went back to ... insisting on their desperate demands and clamoring for a shameful return, renouncing ... the joy which in the space of less than thirty hours God had prepared for them.

But Christopher Columbus ... did not yield to such blameworthy cowardice. ... Rather, with a renewed spirit ... with a more lively hope, more gracious and pleasing words ... and greater promises, he encouraged them to go forward and to persevere. He added, also, that it was useless to complain, since his purpose and that of the sovereigns had been and was to come discover the Indies by way of that western sea; and that the sailors had asked to accompany him for that end, and so his intention was to proceed, with Our Lord's assistance, until he found them; and that they must certainly be nearer the Indies than they thought.

Here I believe that God held his hand, so that they would not commit some such folly as they had often schemed. On Thursday, October 11 ... they saw new signs, more certain and assured than all the others, at which they all breathed again. They navigated toward the west southwest, encountering a higher and rougher sea than any they had experienced during the entire voyage.

They saw sea gulls and, best of all, close to the ship a green branch, as if someone had just severed it from its roots. Those on the caravel *Pinta* saw a stick and a cane; they picked up another little stick shaped, it appeared, by iron, also a piece of cane, a small board, and another land plant. Those on the caravel *Niña* saw other signs, too, and a little branch covered with dogroses, at which all the caravels greatly rejoiced. On this day they went, until sunset, twenty-seven leagues.

Christopher Columbus understood that they were now very near land: first, because of such plain signs; second, because he knew how far he had come from the Canaries toward these parts. For he always had it in mind ... that after he had navigated approximately 750 leagues from the island of Hierro through this Ocean Sea, he would find land.

Therefore, after nightfall, at the time they said the Salve Regina, as is the custom of mariners, he made a very cheerful, gracious address to the whole crew, urging them to consider the blessings which God had bestowed on him and on everyone in that voyage, in giving them so smooth a sea, such gentle, favorable winds, and such calm weather, without the usual storms and headwinds. He said that since he was hoping, through God's mercy, that before many hours passed they would reach land, he asked them earnestly to keep very close watch in the forecastle. ... For besides the gift of 10,000 maravedis which the queen had assigned to the first to sight land, he promised to give that man at once a silk doublet.

Las Casas explains here that although Columbus had instructed his captains not to sail later than midnight after they were 700 leagues beyond the Canaries, his great eagerness made him counteract the instructions now.

This night, after sunset, he navigated toward the west, on the course he had followed ever since leaving the Canaries, and went twelve miles an hour. By two hours after midnight, they would have gone ninety miles, or twenty-two and a half leagues.

While Christopher Columbus was in the sterncastle, keeping a sharper lookout than any other ... because the affair concerned him most of all, he saw a light — although so obscured or clouded that he did not wish to affirm that it was land. But he called Pero Gutiérrez, butler of the king's dais, to him privately, and told him that a light had appeared; that he should look and see what he thought of it. Pero Gutiérrez saw it, and said that it likewise seemed to him to be a light. Christopher Columbus also summoned Rodrigo Sánchez de Segovia, whom the sovereigns had appointed comptroller of the entire fleet, but he could not see it.

Afterward it was seen one or two times, and Christopher Columbus says it was like a little candle that is raised and lowered. He did not doubt that it was a true light, and, consequently, that he was near land — and so it was.

What I make of this is that in these islands, which are temperate and without any cold weather, the Indians leave, or were leaving, their thatch houses, called *bohíos*, at night, to take care of their natural needs. Each carries in his hand a firebrand, pine splinter, or some other very dry, resinous wood; it burns like a torch when the night is dark, and with it they go back and forth. And in this way one could see the light the three or four times that Christopher Columbus and the others saw it.

While Christopher Columbus was watching very closely to sight land and admonishing those watching at the prow of the ship not to be negligent, and as the caravel *Pinta*, under Martín Alonso Pinzón, went ahead of the others because it was faster, land was sighted, about two leagues away, at two hours after midnight. Martín Alonso Pinzón then gave the signals ... he was supposed to give according to his instructions: these were to fire one shot from a lombard, and to run up the flags. And it appears that since land was sighted two hours after midnight, Thursday, this discovery should be set down on Friday; thus it took place on October 12.

A sailor on the *Pinta* named Rodrigo de Triana first sighted land, but the sovereigns ruled that Christopher Columbus should have the 10,000 maravedis annuity, considering that since he had first seen the light, he was the first to sight land. ...

So, land having been sighted, they lowered all sails. The ships remained with only the *papahigo*, which is what mariners call the mainsail, all the bonnets having been taken down, and they went beating back and forth until it was day.

When day came, which was not a little desired by all, the three ships draw near land and let go their anchors. The Spaniards see the shore crowded with naked people. ... This land was, and is, an island approximately fifteen leagues long, all low, without any mountain, like an orchard full of green, cool trees. ... It was called ... Guanahaní, the last syllable long and accented. In the middle of it was a body of fresh water, from which the Indians were accustomed to drink.

The island was inhabited by many people, for whom there was not enough room; for ... all the lands of this world are very pleasant, especially all these islands of the "Lucayos." This is what the people of these small islands call themselves, meaning "inhabitants of *cays*," because *"cays,"* in this language, are islands.

Now the Admiral and all his mariners were eager to land and see these people; and these people were no less eager to see them come forth. They marveled at those ships, which they must have thought were some animals that came over the sea or emerged from it. On Friday, October 12, in the morning, Christopher Columbus left in his armed ship's boat ... with all the crew that could fit into it. He also ordered Captains Martín Alonso and Vincente Yáñez to do the same and depart.

The Admiral took out the royal standard, and the two captains, two banners, each with a green cross. The Admiral carried these banners in all the ships as a sign and device, with an "F" denoting the king, Don Fernando, and an "I" for the queen, Doña Isabella, and above each letter its crown — one at one end of the cross, the other at the other.

Upon landing, the Admiral and all kneel. They give boundless thanks to Almighty God. Many shed tears because He had brought them to safety and was showing them some of the fruits they had so longed and sighed for on such an unusual, extended journey, accompanied by so much toil, hardship, and fear. . . . Who can express and enhance the joy all felt . . . amidst the confusion of those who . . . had not trusted the constant, patient Columbus, but had resisted and injured him? Who can make known the homage they were doing him? The pardon which, with tears, they were asking of him? The offers they were making to serve him all their lives? In short, the endearments, honors, and thanks they were giving him, the obedience and subjection they were promising him? . . .

He, with tears, was embracing them, forgiving them, inciting all to direct all that to God. There his entire company accepted him as admiral and viceroy and governor under the sovereigns of Castile, and rendered him homage . . . with such joy and gladness that it is better to refer the grandeur of the occasion to the discretion of the prudent reader than by inadequate words to seek to manifest it.

Then the Admiral, before the two captains; Rodrigo de Escobedo, secretary of the whole fleet; Rodrigo Sánchez de Segovia, the comptroller; and all the Christian people whom he carried with him, landed and said they should bear witness how, before all of them, he took . . . possession of the said island, which he named San Salvador, for the king and queen, his lords. And he made the solemn declarations which were required, and which are contained at greater length in the depositions set down there in writing.

The great number of Indians who were present were astonished by all these acts. They gazed at the Christians and were awe-struck by their beards, their whiteness, and their clothing. They approached the bearded men, especially the Admiral, as they judged him to be the chief because of his height and authoritative bearing and also because of his scarlet clothes. They touched the beards with their hands, marveling at them, for they have none, and inspected the Christians' white hands and faces very politely.

The Admiral and the others, observing their simplicity, permitted it all with great pleasure. The Christians stood looking at the Indians, marveling no less than the Indians marveled at them—wondering at the Indians' extreme mildness, artlessness, and trust in a people they had never known and might dread and flee because of their fierce appearance.

The Christians also wondered at how the Indians came near and walked so freely among them, as fearless and unsuspicious as if they had been fathers and sons; at how they all went naked, just as their mothers bore them . . . so that they seemed not to have lost, or to have had restored, the state of innocence in which, for a tiny space of time, said not to have exceeded six hours, our father Adam lived.

❧{ 5 }❧

Reception in Barcelona

The following selection, from Book I, Chapter 78, relates Columbus' triumphal return from the New World — his joyous reception by the Catholic sovereigns Ferdinand and Isabella, in Barcelona, April 1493. (Obras Escogidas, I, 232-235.)

After the courier was dispatched, Don Christopher Columbus, now the Admiral, clad in the best attire he could find, departed from Seville, taking the Indians with him. There were seven Indians who remained after past hardships, for the others had died on him. I myself saw them then in Seville; they were lodging near the arch called the Arch of Images, by St. Nicholas. Don Christopher Columbus carried very beautiful, red-tinged green parrots and *guaycas*, which were masks made of a collection of fishbones arranged like pearl-seed, and some belts of the same material, fashioned with admirable craftsmanship; also a great quantity and variety of very fine gold, and many other things never before seen or heard of in Spain.

He hastened from Seville with the Indians and the others. Rumors began to fly through Castile that lands called "the Indies" had been discovered, along with many different peoples and new things, and that the discoverer was coming, by such and such a road, bringing some of the people with him. Then a multitude came out to see him. They came not only from towns through which he was passing, but many villages far from his route emptied; their inhabitants filled the roads ... to march on to the other towns to receive him.

Because of the memorials they had received from Don Christopher Columbus, from Seville, the sovereigns arranged that a beginning should be made in furnishing what was needed for the second voyage, and they wrote Don Juan Rodríguez de Fonseca, archdeacon of Seville. ... This Don Juan de Fonseca, although an ecclesiastic and archdeacon, ... later bishop of Badajoz and Palencia, and in the end of Burgos, in which office he died, was well versed in worldly business, especially in assembling warriors for fleets at sea, which was work more appropriate for Basques than for bishops. For this reason, as long as they lived, the sovereigns always entrusted him with the fleets they assembled. They now ordered him to take charge of preparing a certain number of ships and men, and certain provisions and other things, according to what the Admiral had indicated in his memorials.

Don Christopher Columbus hurried as fast as possible to reach Barcelona, where he arrived in the middle of April—and the sovereigns were very anxious to see him. When it was known that he was arriving, they ordered that he be given a solemn and very beautiful welcome, for which the entire city came out, so that there was not room for all the people in the streets. All wondered to see that venerable person who was said to have discovered another world; to see the Indians, parrots, jewels, and gold things he had discovered and was bringing, things never before seen or heard of.

To receive him with more pomp and splendor, the sovereigns ordered their platform and royal throne with its canopy to be erected in public, where they were seated, and near them the prince, Don Juan. All were very festive; they were accompanied by many great lords — Castilians, Catalans, Valencians, and Aragonese — all eager for the arrival of that one who had accomplished such a great feat, which was a cause of gladness to all Christendom.

Then Don Christopher Columbus entered the square, where the sovereigns were accompanied by a multitude of gentlemen and nobles. Amongst them all, as he had a lofty and authoritative bearing, like that of a Roman senator, his venerable countenance, gray hair, and modest smile stood out, expressing well the joy and glory with which he came.

After he had first shown his deep respect, as was fitting toward such great princes, the sovereigns stood up for him as though for one of their great lords. Then, drawing nearer, he knelt and begged that they give him their hands. They consented and, when their hands had been kissed, with cheerful faces ordered him to rise. And, what was the height of the honor and favor they were wont to bestow on just a few great ones, they commanded that a chair be brought and that he sit before their royal persons.

With great composure and prudence he recounted the favors which God had granted him in his voyage, for the happiness of such Catholic sovereigns. . . . He described the magnitude and blessedness of the lands he had discovered and declared how much more there was to discover, especially in that at that time he considered the island of Cuba mainland. . . . He showed the things he carried, never before seen, taking out the large sample of gold consisting of pieces that had been fashioned, although not highly polished, and of many coarse and fine grains. . . . He asserted the infinite amount of gold shown to be in those lands and his confidence that it would restore the royal treasury—as if he had already collected and deposited it under his keys. And likewise, what was of greater weight and a rare treasure, he described the multitude, simplicity, mildness, nakedness, and certain customs of their peoples, and their fit disposition and capability . . . for being led to our holy Catholic faith. . . .

When they have heard and deeply considered all this, the Catholic and most devout princes arise; they kneel together on the ground, and raising their hands, begin to give thanks to the Creator from the bottom of their hearts, their eyes touched with tears. And since the singers of the chapel royal were provided and prepared, they sing the *Te Deum*. The high-pitched wind instruments respond in such a way that they appeared in that hour to be manifesting and partaking of celestial pleasure.

Who will be able to describe the tears of the sovereigns, of the many great lords, . . . and of all the members of the royal household? What rejoicing, what gladness, what happiness bathed the hearts of all! How they began to encourage one another and to propose in their hearts to come settle these lands, and help convert these peoples! For they heard and saw that the most serene princes, especially the saintly queen, Doña Isabella, . . . gave all to understand that the chief pleasure of their souls came . . . because by their support and expenditures . . . pagan races had been discovered, so numerous and so well disposed that in the sovereigns' time they could come to know their Creator, and be led to the bosom of the holy, universal Church. . . .

Great joys came to their royal hearts while those blessed sovereigns reigned, although, as the crown of their merits, God always mingled with these enough deep sorrows to show his singular care for their betterment. Joys such as the birth of the prince, Don Juan; seeing the cross of Jesus Christ placed in the Alhambra of Granada, when, after such immense hardships, they took that great city and that entire kingdom; the marriages of the most serene infantas, their daughters, especially the marriage of the queen princess; and the birth of the prince, Don Miguel, her son; the coming of the king, Don Philip, who was the prince; the birth of the emperor, Don Carlos, who at present triumphs in the world, son of the said king, Don Philip, and of the queen, our lady Doña Juana, second of the Catholic sovereigns; and other joys which God wished to give them in this life.

But certainly, according to what I have always felt, the joy they received from this miraculous discovery was not much inferior to those others; nay, I believe that it surpassed many of them. . . .

Finally, the most serene sovereigns give the Admiral permission, for that day, to go rest in his lodgings, to which, at the command of the sovereign, he was honorably escorted by the whole court.

❧{ 6 }❧

The Conquest of Cuba

The following selection, from Book III, Chapters 26, 29, and 30, describes Las Casas' part in the conquest of Cuba, which took place in 1511-1513, under Diego Velázquez. Las Casas went as a chaplain with an old friend, Pánfilo de Narváez Velázquez' lieutenant. (Obras Escogidas, II, 236-237, 243-246.)

At this time, when it was known in the island of Jamaica that Diego Velázquez had gone to settle and pacify . . the island of Cuba, Juan de Esquivel, the deputy in Jamaica, agreed to send one Pánfilo de Narváez, a native of Valladolid with thirty Spaniards, to aid Diego Velázquez—or else they bestirred themselves and asked permission to go there. All were archers, with their bows and arrows, in the use of which they were more practiced than the Indians.

This Pánfilo de Narváez was a man with an air of authority, tall of stature, and rather fair-haired, tending toward red. He was honorable and wise, but not very prudent; good company, with good habits, valiant in fighting against the Indians and would perhaps have been valiant against other peoples—but above all he had this defect, that he was very careless.

With his band of bowmen he was well received by Diego Velázquez. . . . Velázquez promptly gave them shares of Indians, as if these were heads of cattle, so that the Indians would serve them, although they had brought some Jamaican Indians to do that wherever they went. Diego Velázquez made this Narváez his chief captain and always honored him in such a way that, after Velázquez, Narváez held first place in that island.

A few days later I went there, the said Diego Velázquez having sent for me because of our past friendship in this island of Hispaniola. We went together, Narváez and I, for about two years, and secured the rest of that island, to the detriment of all of it, as will be seen.

Las Casas tells how Velázquez terrorized the natives of eastern Cuba, near Cape Maisi, executed the chieftain Hatuey (see p. 147 below), and went on to Baracoa. Narváez landed at the Gulf of Guacayanabo, on the south coast near Maisi, and, on orders from Velázquez invaded the province of Camagüey, in central Cuba.

The Spaniards entered the province of Camagüey which is large and densely populated ... and when they reached the villages, the inhabitants had prepared as well as they could cassava bread from their food; what they called *guaminiquinajes* from their hunting; and also fish, if they had caught any.

Immediately upon arriving at a village, the cleric Casas would have all the little children band together; taking two or three Spaniards to help him, along with some sagacious Indians of this island of Hispaniola, whom he had brought with him, and a certain servant of his, he would baptize the children he found in the village. He did this throughout the island ... and there were many for whom God provided holy baptism because He had predestined them to glory. God provided it at a fitting time, for none or almost none of those children remained alive after a few months. ...

When the Spaniards arrived at a village and found the Indians at peace in their houses, they did not fail to injure and scandalize them. Not content with what the Indians freely gave, they took their wretched subsistence from them, and some, going further, chased after their wives and daughters, for this is and always has been the Spaniards' common custom in these Indies. Because of this and the urging of the said father, Captain Narvéz ordered that after the father had separated all the inhabitants of the village in half the houses, leaving the other half empty for the Spaniards' lodging, no one should dare go to the Indians' section. For this purpose, the father would go ahead with three or four men and reach a village early; by the time the Spaniards came, he had already gathered the Indians in one part and cleared the other.

Thus, because the Indians saw that the father did things for them, defending and comforting them, and also baptizing their children, in which affairs he seemed to have more command and authority than others, he received much respect and credit throughout the island among the Indians. Further, they honored him as they did their priests, magicians, prophets, or physicians, who were all one and the same.

Because of this . . . it became unnecessary to go ahead of the Spaniards. He had only to send an Indian with an old piece of paper on a stick, informing them through the messenger that those letters said thus and so. That is, that they should all be calm, that no one should absent himself because he would do them no harm, that they should have food prepared for the Christians and their children ready for baptism, or that they should gather in one part of the village, and anything else that it seemed good to counsel them — and that if they did not carry these things out, the father would be angry, which was the greatest threat that could be sent them.

They performed everything with a very good will, to the best of their ability. And great was the reverence and fear which they had for the letters, for they saw that through these what was being done in other, distant regions was known. It seemed more than a miracle to them. . . .

The Spaniards thus passed through certain villages of that province on the road they were taking. And because the folk of the villages . . . were eager to see such a new people and especially to see the three or four mares being taken there, at which the whole land was frightened — news of them flew through the island — many came to look at them in a large town called Caonao, the penultimate syllable long. And the Spaniards, on the morning of the day they arrived at the town, stopped to breakfast in a riverbed that was dry but for a few small pools. This riverbed was full of whetstones, and all longed to sharpen their swords on them [and did]. When they had finished their breakfast, they continued on the road to Caonao.

Along the road for two or three leagues there was an arid plain, where one found oneself thirsty after any work; and there certain Indians from the villages brought them some gourds of water, and some things to eat.

They arrived at the town of Caonao in the evening. Here they found many people, who had prepared a great deal of food consisting of cassava bread and fish, because they had a large river close by and also were near the sea. In a little square were 2,000 Indians, all squatting because they have this custom, all staring, frightened, at the mares. Nearby was a large *bohío*, or large house, in which were more than 500 other Indians, close-packed and fearful, who did not dare come out.

When some of the domestic Indians the Spaniards were taking with them as servants (who were more than 1,000 souls . . .) wished to enter the large house, the Cuban Indians had chickens ready and said to them: "Take these — do not enter here." For they already knew that the Indians who served the Spaniards were not apt to perform any other deeds than those of their masters.

There was a custom among the Spaniards that one person, appointed by the captain, should be in charge of distributing to each Spaniard the food and other things the Indians gave. And while the captain was thus on his mare and the others mounted on theirs, and the father himself was observing how the bread and fish were distributed, a Spaniard, in whom the devil is thought to have clothed himself, suddenly drew his sword. Then the whole hundred drew theirs and began to rip open the bellies, to cut and kill those lambs — men, women, children, and old folk, all of whom were seated, off guard and frightened, watching the mares and the Spaniards. And within two credos, not a man of all of them there remains alive.

The Spaniards enter the large house nearby, for this was happening at its door, and in the same way, with cuts and stabs, begin to kill as many as they found there, so that a stream of blood was running, as if a great number of cows had perished. Some of the Indians who could make haste climbed up the poles and woodwork of the house to the top, and thus escaped.

The cleric had withdrawn shortly before this massacre to where another small square of the town was formed, near where they had lodged him. This was in a large house where all the Spaniards also had to stay, and here about forty of the Indians who had carried the Spaniards' baggage from the provinces farther back were stretched out on the ground, resting. And five Spaniards chanced to be with the cleric. When these heard the blows of the swords and knew that the Spaniards were killing the Indians—without seeing anything, because there were certain houses between—they put hands to their swords and are about to kill the forty Indians . . . to pay them their commission.

The cleric, moved to wrath, opposes and rebukes them harshly to prevent them, and having some respect for him, they stopped what they were going to do, so the forty were left alive. The five go to kill where the others were killing. And as the cleric had been detained in hindering the slaying of the forty carriers, when he went he found a heap of dead, which the Spaniards had made among the Indians, which was certainly a horrible sight.

When Narváez, the captain, saw him he said: "How does Your Honor like what these our Spaniards have done?"

Seeing so many cut to pieces before him, and very upset at such a event, the cleric replied: "That I commend you and them to the devil!"

The heedless Naváez remained, still watching the slaughter as it took place, without speaking, acting, or moving any more than if he had been marble. For if he had wished, being on horseback and with a lance in his hands, he could have prevented the Spaniards from killing even ten persons.

Then the cleric leaves him, and goes elsewhere through some groves seeking Spaniards to stop them from killing. For they were passing through the groves looking for someone to kill, sparing neither boy, child, woman, nor old person. And they did more, in that certain Spaniards went to the road to the river, which was nearby. Then all the Indians who had escaped with wounds, stabs, and cuts—all who could flee to throw themselves into the river to save themselves—met with the Spaniards who finished them.

Another outrage occurred which should not be left untold,

so that the deeds of our Christians in these regions may be observed. When the cleric entered the large house where I said there were about 500 souls — or whatever the number, which was great — and saw with horror the dead there and those who had escaped above by the poles or woodwork, he said to them:

"No more, no more. Do not be afraid. There will be no more, there will be no more."

With this assurance, believing that it would be thus, an Indian descended, a well-disposed young man of twenty-five or thirty years, weeping. And as the cleric did not rest but went everywhere to stop the killing, the cleric then left the house. And just as the young man came down, a Spaniard who was there drew a cutlass or half sword and gives him a cut through the loins, so that his intestines fall out.

The Indian, moaning, takes his intestines in his hands and comes fleeing out of the house. He encounters the cleric . . . and the cleric tells him some things about the faith, as much as the time and anguish permitted, explaining to him that if he wished to be baptized he would go to heaven to live with God. The sad one, weeping and showing pain as if he were burning in flames, said yes, and with this the cleric baptized him. He then fell dead on the ground.

Of all that has been said, I am a witness. I was present and saw it; and I omit many other particulars in order to shorten the account.

❈{ 7 }❈

Magellan and His Globe

The following selection from Book III, Chapter 101, describes Ferdinand Magellan, whom Las Casas saw at the Spanish court in 1518, just after Magellan came there from Portugal. Magellan offered Spaniards a western route to the Spice Islands, which he said would enable them to compete with the Portuguese, who went east by way of the Cape of Good Hope. (Obras Escogidas, II, 415-416.)

At this time, there came fleeing—or secretly—from Portugal to Valladolid, because of a certain grievance he held against the Portuguese king, a man called Ferdinand Magellan, "Margalhães" in Portuguese. He was a mariner, or at least knew much of the sea. With him was a bachelor of arts, or one who said he was a bachelor of arts, named Rui Faleiro. By his own showing, he was a great astrologer, but the Portuguese declared that he was possessed by a devil and knew nothing of astrology.

These two offered to prove that the Moluccas and other islands from which the Portuguese bring spices to Portugal fell within the demarcation or division of southern and western regions, which had been begun, but not finished, between the Catholic sovereigns of Castile and King Don Juan II of Portugal. They would discover a route to the Moluccas beyond the route the Portuguese took, and this would be through a certain strait, of which they knew.

They came with this news first to the bishop of Burgos, as

they understood that until then he had governed the Indies, although at this period he was like a disarmed galley. The bishop took them to the grand chancellor, and the grand chancellor spoke to the king and to Monsieur de Chièvres.

Magellan was carrying a well-painted globe, on which the whole world was depicted. On it he indicated the route he proposed to take, except that he left the strait blank on purpose, so that no one would steal the knowledge of it from him. And on that day and at that hour, I found myself in the chamber of the grand chancellor, when the bishop brought the globe and showed the grand chancellor the voyage which was to be made.

And when I spoke to Magellan and asked him what route he planned to take, he answered that he must go by way of Cape Santa María, which we call the Río de la Plata, and from there sail up to the coast until he hit the strait.

"But suppose you do not find the strait by which you have to pass to the other sea?" I then asked.

He answered that if he did not find it, he would go by the route the Portuguese took. But according to a letter written by an Italian gentleman named [Antonio] Pigafetta, a Venetian who went on that voyage of discovery with Magellan, Magellan was confident that he was going to find the strait. For he says that Magellan had seen the strait, drawn as he found it, on a navigation chart made by one Martin of Bohemia, a great pilot and cosmographer, in the treasury of the king of Portugal. And because the strait was located on the seacoast and in country within the bounds of the sovereigns of Castile, he had to bestir himself and come offer the king of Castile the discovery of a new route to the said Moluccas and other islands.

This Ferdinand Magellan must have been a man of spirit, valiant both in his thinking and in his undertaking of great things, although he did not have an imposing presence; for he was small in stature and did not seem to be much. But neither did he give the impression that he lacked prudence and that anyone whatever could easily overcome him, because he appeared circumspect and courageous.

A Portuguese history relates that when two ships left India for the kingdom of Portugal, Magellan in one of them, both ran aground on some shoals and were lost. But the people all saved themselves, and also many of the provisions, in ships' boats, landing on a nearby islet. They agreed that they would go in the boats to a certain port, in India, so many leagues away.

However, since there was not room for all in the boats, . . . there was great strife over who should go in the first ferrying. The captains, gentlemen, and chief persons wished to be first; the mariners and low people said no, they should go.

When Magellan saw the dangerous dispute and the peril they were in, he said: "Let the captains and gentlemen go, and I will remain with the mariners and the others—provided you give us your word, and swear to send for us immediately upon your arrival."

The mariners and low people said that if Magellan remained with them, they were content to stay. At this moment, Magellan was in one of the boats. Now that they wished to leave, one of the mariners who was staying thought Magellan was dissembling in order to depart, and said:

"Señor, didn't you promise to remain with us?"

"Yes," Magellan answered. No sooner said than done—he jumps from the boat to the shore. "You see—here I am!"

And thus he stayed with them and showed himself to be a man of truth and courage. He must also have been a man of rank, since all those low people were satisfied to remain with him and were pacified; and he stopped their wrangling, which would have endangered all.

⊰{ 8 }⊱

The Character of Cortés

The following selection, from Book III, Chapters 27 and 115, gives Las Casas' impression of Hernando Cortés, whom he knew, and tells how Cortés departed from Cuba on November 18, 1518, for the conquest of Mexico against Diego Velázquez's wishes. (Obras Escogidas, *II, 239-240, 450-451.*)

Diego Velázquez had two secretaries: one, this Hernando Cortés, and the other, Andrés de Duero, no bigger than your thumb, but prudent, very discreet, and a good penman. Cortés had an advantage over him in being a Latinist, simply because he had studied law at Salamanca and was a bachelor of law. Otherwise, Cortés was a talker and a wit, more communicative with others than Duero was and thus not so fit to be a secretary. He affected learning and was circumspect, although he did not reveal that he knew as much or was as capable as he afterward showed himself to be in difficult situations. He was a native of Medellín, son of a squire I knew, who was very poor and humble, although an Old Christian and, it is said, a nobleman. . . .

The malcontents found this Cortés ready to carry their complaints, letters, and communications [to the appellate court in Hispaniola], perhaps because he too was discontented with his master, Diego Velázquez. As he was about to embark with his papers in an Indian canoe, Diego Velázquez was informed and had him seized; he wanted to hang him. Many persons pleaded for him. Velázquez ordered him thrown into a ship, to be sent as a prisoner to this island of Hispaniola. Somehow Cortés freed himself from the ship, got into a boat at night, came to the church, and was there on a certain day. One Juan Escudero, a marshal (whom he afterward hanged in New Spain), bided his time, and when Cortés took a walk outside the church, apprehended him.

Diego Velázquez's anger increased, and he held Cortés prisoner for many days. But in the end (Diego Velázquez had a good disposition and his annoyance did not last long), what with many persons asking him to pardon Cortés, he had to do it. However, he did not wish to turn around and take him back into his service as secretary.

Gómara, the cleric who wrote the *History* of Cortés and who lived with him in Castile after he was a marquis—who saw nothing in the Indies nor was ever there, and did not write anything except what Cortés himself told him—invents many things in Cortés' favor which are certainly not true. Among other things, speaking in the beginning of the conquest of Mexico, says that Cortés was angry and did not wish to talk to Diego Velázquez for many days. He says that one night Cortés went armed to where Diego Velázquez was alone except for his servants; that he entered the house and that Diego Velázquez was afraid when he saw him armed, at such an hour; that Velázquez asked him to dine and rest, and Cortés replied that he came only to learn what complaints Velázquez had against him, and to satisfy him and be his friend and servant; and that they clasped hands as friends and both slept in the same bed that night. This is all a big lie. . . .

I myself saw Cortés in those days, or shortly after. He was so abject and humble that he would have sought the favor of the least of Diego Velázquez' servants. And Diego Velázquez was not so lacking in choler, nor even of so little seriousness, but that . . . had he perceived one pin-prick of pride and presumption in Cortés, he would either have hanged him or at least have cast him out of the land and overwhelmed him so that he would never again in his life raise his head.

After Diego Velázquez decided to establish towns or villas of Spaniards in the provinces of that island, Cuba, and distributed the Indians to certain inhabitants, as the history will tell, since he had lost all his anger at Cortés, he also gave him Indians and his right of domicile, and treated him well. He honored him by making him the *alcaide* [governor] in the villa, afterward the city, of Santiago, where he had enrolled him. For Diego Velázquez was certainly of this nature: that, as a man who was not vindictive but practiced kindness, once the first fit of passion was over he forgave everything. On his side, too, Cortés was not careless about serving and pleasing Velázquez, not angering him in small things or great, for Cortés was very astute. Thus he won Velázquez back completely, then neglected him as before.

Cortés had a son or daughter, I don't know whether by his wife, and he begged Diego Velázquez to consent to raise the child from the baptismal font and be its godfather. Out of good will, and to honor Cortés, Velázquez agreed to this. . . .

I said that he had a wife—it was thus. In the time of his disfavor, Cortés married a maiden (although Gómara seems to say that he had her first as his mistress), the sister of one Juan Suárez, a native of Granada. They had gone to Cuba with their mother, poor folks, and it appears that Cortés must have promised to marry her and afterward refused. Gómara says that Diego Velázquez had a bad opinion of him because he did not wish to keep his word and marry her; and that was not unreasonable or unjust, since Velázquez was the governor—or even if he had not been. So Cortés married in the end and was no richer than his wife; and in those days of his poverty, humility, and low position I heard him say—I was with him and he said it to me—that he was as satisfied with her as if she had been the daughter of a duchess.

Now let us see how Hernando Cortés hastened from the island of Cuba, and with what justice he started. . . . When Diego Velázquez had been persuaded by Amador de Lares, or had persuaded himself, to name Cortés captain general of the expedition to Mexico . . . Diego Velázquez pressed forward in Cortés' expedition with great urgency. Nor was Cortés asleep. Every day, Diego Velázquez went to the port on horseback, although it was nearby, and Cortés and the whole city with him, to see the ships and hasten everything that had to be done.

One time, Cortés was going there and Diego Velázquez's

clown, named Francisquillo, was going ahead uttering jests, for he was accustomed to do that, and among other witticisms, turning his face toward Diego Velázquez, he said to him: "Ah, Diego!"

"What do you want, madman?" Diego Velázquez responds.

"Watch your step, so that we won't have to go and hunt for Cortés," Francisquillo adds.

Diego Velázquez then shouts with laughter and says to Cortés, who was at his right hand because he was *alcaide* of the city and had already been chosen captain: *"Compadre"* (For he always called him that), "see what that rogue of a Francisquillo says."

"What, señor?" replied Cortés, although he had heard it. But he pretended that he was talking to another person near him.

"That we will have to go and hunt for you," says Diego Velázquez.

"Forget it, your honor—that's a mad rogue," Cortés answered. Then he said to Francisquillo: "I tell you, madman, that if I catch you, watch out for what will happen!"

All this took place with everyone mocking and laughing. But as Diego Velázquez went in haste about this business, either because the folly—or, better said, the prudent judgment and prophecy—of the madman Francisquillo pricked his soul or because his friends and relatives . . . pointed out . . . the great mistake he was making in trusting Cortés . . . and that it was probable and even certain that Cortés would rebel . . . , Diego Velázquez decided to relieve Cortés of the office. . . .

And since, as has been said, Diego Velázquez informed the king's officials, especially the paymaster Amador de Lares, about affairs of government and of those fleets, faith was not kept as it should have been. According to what is believed, Amador de Lares must have revealed it to Cortés; and if the partnership and league said to exist between them really did exist, it was no wonder that Amador, in his own interest, should notify him. In short, in one way or another, Cortés succeeded in finding out. Considering his quickness and knowledge of the world, it was not necessary for him to do more than see Diego Velázquez's face.

The first night that Cortés understood, after Diego Velázquez had gone to bed and all in his palace had departed in the deepest silence of the night, Cortés goes with great diligence to wake those most his friends and told them that now was a fit time to embark. And when he had chosen a company of them that he thought adequate to defend his person, he goes from there to the meat market. Although it grieved the butcher, who was obliged to provide meat for the whole city, Cortés takes all, not leaving any cattle, swine, or sheep, and has it carried to the ships.

He demands, though not in a loud voice, because if he had shouted perhaps it would have cost him his life, that they not punish the butcher for not providing meat for the city. Then he removed a small gold chain which he wore around his neck and gave it to the contractor or butcher. Cortés himself told me this.

Cortés then goes to the ships to embark, with all the people he could wake without an outcry. Many of those who had to go with him, and who went, were already on board. When he had left, Diego Velázquez was informed, either by the butchers or by other persons who perceived his going, how Cortés had departed and was already aboard the ships. Diego Velázquez rises and rides to the seashore as the day dawns; the whole city, dismayed, goes with him.

As soon as Cortés saw them, he has a boat prepared with artillery, shotguns or arquebuses, crossbows, and the weapons that suit him and the people he most trusts. And carrying his alcaide's staff, he comes in the boat to within a crossbow shot of land, and stops there.

"Compadre," Diego Velázquez addresses him, "why are you leaving like this? Is this a good way to say good-bye?"

"Señor, your honor must pardon me," Cortés answered, "because these and similar things have to be done before they are thought upon. Your honor may see who commands me."

Observing Cortés' disloyalty and effrontery, Diego Velázquez had nothing to say in reply.

Cortés orders the boat to turn back, and he returns to the ships. In great haste, he orders the sails raised; and with very few provisions, because the ships were still not loaded, he departed from there, November 18, 1518.

PART II

AUTOBIOGRAPHER

Autobiography in the History of the Indies

Las Casas severely represses mention of himself in his writings. However, he does play a role in the *History of the Indies*, in the protest movement against the Spanish mistreatment of the Indians. He relates his conversion, his struggles at court for the Indians, the Jeronymite investigation of conditions in the New World, the attempt to recruit farmer-emigrants for the Indies, the failure of his colony in Venezuela, and his entry into the Dominican Order.

Although Las Casas was a key figure in every one of these projects, he refers to himself simply as "the cleric" and gives no personal details. Nevertheless, the perceptive reader may deduce certain traits, such as alertness, self-confidence, and determination, even enjoyment of a foe's discomfiture, from the action in the following passages. All are taken from the *History of the Indies*.

✥{ 9 }✥

"Are Not the Indians Men?"

The following selection, from Book III, Chapters 4 and 5, contains no reference to Las Casas but presents the beginning of the Dominicans' campaign against Indian slavery in Hispaniola. However, Las Casas may well have heard one or both of the sensational sermons preached by Fray Antonio de Montesinos in December 1511, and described below; in any event, he was soon to be profoundly influenced by the Dominicans' ideas. (Obras Escogidas, II, 176-179)

When Sunday and the hour to preach arrived, ... Father Fray Antonio de Montesinos ascended the pulpit and took as the text and foundation of his sermon, which he carried written out and signed by the other friars: "I am the voice of the one crying in the desert." After he completed his introduction and said something concerning the subject of Advent, he began to emphasize the aridity in the desert of Spanish consciences in this island, and the ignorance in which they lived; also, in what danger of eternal damnation they were, from taking no notice of the grave sins in which, with such apathy, they were immersed and dying.

Then he returns to his text, speaking thus: "I have ascended here to cause you to know those sins, I who am the voice of Christ in the desert of this island. Therefore it is fitting that you listen to this voice, not with careless attention, but with all your heart and, senses. For this voice will be the strangest you ever

heard, the harshest and hardest, most fearful and most dangerous you ever thought to hear."

This voice cried out for some time, with very combative and
terrible words, so that it made their flesh tremble, and they
seemed already standing before the divine judgment. Then, in
a grand manner, the voice . . . declared what it was, or what that
divine inspiration consisted of: "This voice," he said, "declares
that you are all in mortal sin, and live and die in it, because of
the cruelty and tyranny you practice among these innocent peoples.

"Tell me, by what right or justice do you hold these Indians
in such a cruel and horrible servitude? On what authority have
you waged such detestable wars against these peoples, who dwelt
quietly and peacefully on their own land? Wars in which you
have destroyed such infinite numbers of them by homicides and
slaughters never before heard of? Why do you keep them so
oppressed and exhausted, without giving them enough to eat or
curing them of the sicknesses they incur from the excessive labor
you give them, and they die, or rather, you kill them, in order
to extract and acquire gold every day?

"And what care do you take that they should be instructed
in religion, so that they may know their God and creator, may
be baptized, may hear Mass, and may keep Sundays and feast
days? Are these not men? Do they not have rational souls? Are
you not bound to love them as you love yourselves? Don't you
understand this? Don't you feel this? Why are you sleeping in
such a profound and lethargic slumber? Be assured that in your
present state you can no more be saved than the Moors or Turks,
who lack the faith of Jesus Christ and do not desire it."

In brief, the voice explained what it had emphasized before
in such a way that it left them astonished—many numb as if
without feeling, others more hardened than before, some somewhat penitent, but none, as I afterward understood, converted.

When the sermon was concluded, Antonio de Montesinos
descended from the pulpit with his head not at all low, for he
was not a man who would want to show fear—as he felt none—
if he displeased his hearers by doing and saying what seemed
fitting to him, according to God. With his companion he goes to
his thatch house where, perhaps, they had nothing to eat but

cabbage broth without olive oil, as sometimes happened. But after he departed, the church remains full of murmurs so that, as I believe, they scarcely permitted the Mass to be finished. One may indeed suppose that a reading from the *Contempt of the World* was not given at everyone's table that day.

After finishing their meal, which must not have been very appetizing, the whole city gathers at the house of the Admiral, Don Diego Columbus . . . , especially the king's officials, the treasurer and auditor, factor and comptroller. They agree to go rebuke and frighten the preacher and the others, if not to punish him as a scandalous man, sower of a new and unheard of doctrine which condemned them all. . . .

They call at the porter's box; the porter opens; they tell him to call the vicar and the friar who had preached such wild things. The vicar, the venerable Father Fray Pedro de Córdoba, emerges alone. They tell him, with more haughtiness than humility, to have the preacher called. Being very prudent, he replies that there was no need; that if his lordship and their worships command something, he was the superior of these religious and would respond. They insist violently that he have the preacher called; he very discreetly . . . excused himself and evaded their request.

Finally . . . when the Admiral and the others saw that the father vicar was not persuaded by arguments and words of high authority, they began to soften, to humble themselves, and to entreat him to order that the preacher be called because, with the vicar present, they wish to talk to them and ask why and on what grounds they had decided to preach something so novel and injurious, in disservice to the king and harmful to all the inhabitants of that city and of this whole island.

When the saintly man saw that they were taking another road and moderating the vigor with which they had come, he ordered the said Father Fray Antonio de Montesinos called. . . . After all were seated, the Admiral presents . . . their complaint. He asks why that father had dared preach things in such disservice to the king and so harmful to that whole land, by affirming that they could not possess Indians after the king, the lord of all the Indies, gave them to them — especially since the Spaniards had won those islands with great hardships and had subjugated the pagans who held them. And since that sermon had been so scandalous ... they had decided that that father should retract everything he had said; if not, they would undertake to arrange a fitting remedy.

The father vicar replied that what that father had preached had been in accord with the vicar's own opinion and desire, and with that of all the others, and had had their assent, after being carefully considered. ... They were obligated to this by divine precept, through their profession in baptism, first as Christians and afterward as Friars Preachers of the truth. In this they intended no disservice to the king, who had sent them here to preach what they felt they should in accordance with the needs of souls, but they intended to serve him faithfully; and they considered it certain that as soon as His Highness was clearly informed of what was happening here, and of what they had preached about it, he would think himself well served and would thank them.

The speech and the reasons given by the saintly man availed little to satisfy them ... , for if they were deprived of their Indians, they would be defrauded of all their sighs and desires for riches. So each one there, especially the heads, said what he fancied to the purpose. All agreed that on the following Sunday that father should retract what he had preached; and they reached such a point of blind ignorance that they said if the friars did not do it, they should pack up in their little thatch houses and embark for Spain.

The father vicar replied: "Certainly, sirs, we will be able to do that with little labor." And it was so indeed, for their valuables were nothing but their coarse frieze habits ... and some blankets of the same frieze. ... Their beds were certain rods placed over some forked poles, called beds of branches, with some handfuls of straw over them. As for certain psalters and the things needed for Mass, room could perhaps have been found for all those in two chests.

Seeing how little God's servants feared all kinds of threats made against them, the officials softened again, beseeching them to reconsider the matter and, having carefully done so, to emend what had been said in another sermon—this to satisfy the community, which had been, and was, greatly scandalized. At last

... in order to rid themselves of the officials and to put an end to their frivolous importunities, the fathers conceded that at a seasonable time it would be thus: the same Father Fray Antonio de Montesinos would return to preach the next Sunday and would go back to the subject and say what seemed best to him about it, and, as much as possible, would try to satisfy them and explain everything he had said. This having been agreed upon, the officials departed, happy in this hope.

They then proclaimed, or some of them did, that they had left with an agreement with the vicar and the others that on the following Sunday that friar would retract everything he had said. And to hear this second sermon no invitations were needed, for there was not a person in the whole city who was not found in the church on that day. . . .

When the hour for the sermon came, after Antonio de Montesinos ascended the pulpit, the text given as the basis of his retraction was a saying from St. Job, Chapter 36, which commences: "I will go back over my knowledge from the beginning, and I will prove that my discourse is without falsehood." That is, "I will go back to rehearse from the beginning my knowledge and the truths which I preached to you last Sunday, and I will show that those words of mine which embittered you are true."

Upon hearing this text of his, the most clear-sighted saw immediately where he was going to end, and it was misery enough to allow him to go on from there. He began to . . . corroborate with more arguments and texts what he had affirmed before, that those oppressed and exhausted peoples were held unjustly and tyrannically. He repeated his understanding that the Spaniards could certainly not be saved in the state they were in, and that therefore they should in time heal themselves. He made them know that the friars would not confess a man of them, any more than they would confess highway robbers, and that the Spaniards might proclaim and write that to whomever they wished in Castile. In all this, the friars considered it certain that they were serving God and doing the king no small favor.

After the sermon was finished, Antonio de Montesinos went to his house. And all the people in the church remained agitated, grumbling, and much angrier at the friars than before, finding themselves defrauded of their vain and wicked hope that what had been said would be unsaid—as if, after the friar made his retraction, the law of God which they disobeyed by oppressing and exterminating these peoples would be changed.

⊰⊱ 10 ⊰⊱

The Conversion of Las Casas

The following selection, from Book III, Chapters 79 and 80, relates Las Casas' change, in the spring of 1514 from a humane and prosperous encomendero to a lifetime crusader for the Indians. Earlier, he had been troubled by the Spanish massacre of Indians at Caonao (see pp. 51-53). (Obras Escogidas, II, 356-360.)

The cleric Bartolomé de las Casas ... was going about preoccupied with his enterprises. Like the others, he was sending Indians of his *repartimiento* [encomienda] to the mines to extract gold, and to the fields to sow, and he was profiting by them as much as he could, although he always took care to support them as well as possible, to treat them gently, and to sympathize with their miseries. But he gave no more consideration than the others to remembering that they were pagan men and to the duty he had to provide them with religious instruction and bring them within the pale of Christ's Church.

Diego Velázquez ... left the port of Xagua to establish a town of Spaniards in the province, where one called Espíritu Santo was founded. And since, except for one in the town of Baracoa, there was not a cleric or friar in the whole island but the said Bartolomé de las Casas, when Pentecost came [Las Casas] decided to leave his house on the river Arimao ... where he had his estate and go say Mass and preach that Pentecost in Espíritu Santo.

Studying the sermons he had preached last Pentecost, or other sermons for that time, he began to turn over in his mind certain texts of Holy Scripture. And if I have not forgotten, the principal one was from Ecclesiasticus, Chapter 34:

> Tainted his gifts who offers in sacrifice ill-gotten goods; mock presents from the lawless win not God's favor. The Lord is the salvation of those sustaining themselves in the way of truth and justice. The Most High approves not the gifts of the godless, nor does he have regard for the offerings of the wicked; nor for their many sacrifices does he forgive their sins. Like the man who slays his neighbor is he who offers sacrifice from the possessions of the poor. He who sheds blood and he who defrauds his servant are brothers.

He began, I say, to reflect on the misery and servitude that those peoples suffered. In this connection, what he had heard and experienced in this island of Hispaniola benefited him — the preaching of the Dominicans that Spaniards could not in good conscience possess Indians, and that the Dominicans did not wish to confess and absolve those who held Indians, which the said cleric did not accept.

And once, while he possessed Indians in this island of Hispaniola, as thoughtlessly and ignorantly as later in the island of Cuba, he wanted to confess to a Dominican whom he found in a certain place. But the Dominican did not wish to confess him. When he asked why not and was given a reason, the cleric refuted it with frivolous arguments and vain solutions, although with a certain seeming probability, so that the Dominican said to him: "I have concluded, father, that truth always encounters much opposition and a lie has many helpers."

The cleric then yielded, because of the reverence and honor he owed the religious, who was a venerable and very learned person, much more learned than the father cleric. But as for giving up his Indians, the cleric didn't care for his opinion.

So it was worth a great deal to him to remember that dispute of his, and even the declaration he had made to the religious, in order to attain a better view of the ignorance and danger he was in, holding Indians like the others and not hesitating to confess those who possessed them or intended to possess them. . . .

After he had spent a few days with these thoughts and had each day become more and more sure, from what he read of [natural and divine] law, and from the events he witnessed — applying the first to the second — he decided for himself, convinced by truth, that everything done to the Indians in these Indies was unjust and tyrannical. He found that all he read tended to confirm this, and he was accustomed to assert that, from the first hour when he began to dispel the darkness of that ignorance, he never read a book in Latin or Spanish — and there were an infinite number in forty-four years — in which he did not find either an argument or a text to prove and corroborate the justice of these Indian peoples and to condemn the injustices, wrongs, and injuries done them.

Finally, he decided to preach that. And in order to freely condemn the repartimientos or encomiendas as unjust and tyrannical, and because if he retained his Indians he would then have in his hand a reproof of his sermons, he decided to give up his Indians and surrender them into the hands of the governor, Diego Velázquez. Not that they would be better off in Velázquez's power, for the cleric treated them with more compassion . . . and he knew that if he relinquished them they must be given to an oppressor. . . . But as . . . he would never escape defamations like "After all, he has Indians; why doesn't he give them up since he asserts it is tyrannical to hold them?" he decided to surrender them completely.

For all this to be better understood, it is well to recall here the partnership and close friendship between this father and one Pedro de Rentería, a prudent man and a very good Christian. . . . As they were not only friends but partners in their estate, and both had their repartimientos of Indians combined, they agreed between themselves that Pedro de la Rentería should go to the island of Jamaica, where he had a brother, to bring back swine to raise and maize to sow, and other things they did not have in Cuba. . . . And for this journey they chartered one of the king's caravels for 2,000 castellanos.

Now as Pedro de la Rentería was absent and the father cleric had decided to give up his Indians and preach what he felt he ought to . . . , he went one day to the governor, Diego Velázquez, and told him what he felt about his own condition, the governor's, and that of the others. He declared that they could not be saved in that state, and that to escape from the danger and do his duty by his office, he intended to preach this. Therefore, he had decided to surrender his Indians to him. . . . So Velázquez could consider them unclaimed and do with them what he would.

But the cleric asked him as a favor to keep that a secret and not to give the Indians to someone else until Rentería returned from his stay on the island of Jamaica. For the Indians and the estate, which both held indivisibly, would suffer loss if someone to whom Velázquez gave the father's Indians should undertake them and the estate before Rentería came.

The governor was perfectly astounded at hearing such a novel and, as it were, monstrous matter. First, because the cleric . . . was of the opinion of the Dominican friars, who had first brought up that business, and that he should dare proclaim it. Second, that he should so justify it and should have such contempt for temporal wealth when he was so well prepared to become rich shortly. . . . And the governor said to him: "Reflect on what you are doing, father, lest you repent. For by God I would wish to see you rich and prosperous, and therefore I do not accept your relinquishing your Indians. And that you may think better of it, I give you fifteen days to consider it carefully, after which you may return to tell me what you decide."

The father cleric replied: "Sir, I receive great honor from your desiring my prosperity, along with the other kindnesses that your honor does me. But count the fifteen days past. And please God, if I repent of this purpose that I have made known to you, and wish to possess Indians, and if you because of your love for me want to entrust or give them to me anew . . . , may it be God who will severely punish you and not forgive you this sin. I only ask your honor that all this may be secret and that you do not give the Indians to anyone until Rentería comes, so that his estate will not be damaged."

So Velázquez promised him that and kept his promise. And from then on he had much more respect for the said cleric. . . .

And all the others in the island began to hold a new concept of him, different from what they had held before, as soon as they knew that he had given up his Indians—something considered, then and always, as the strongest possible evidence of saintliness. So great was, and is, the ignorance of those who have come to these parts.

This secret was revealed in this way. The said cleric preached on the day of the Assumption of Our Lady, in that aforementioned place Espíritu Santo, and discussed the active and contemplative lives, the subject of the Gospel for that day, touching on the spiritual and temporal acts of charity. It was then necessary for him to show them their duty to carry out and perform these acts among those peoples, by whom they were so cruelly profiting, and to reprove their neglect and omission of these acts. For this, it became pertinent to reveal the secret agreement that he had made with the governor, and he said: "Sir, I give you license to tell everyone you want to what we agreed on in secret. And I will permit myself to tell it to those who are present."

Having said this, he began to declare their ignorance, and the injustices, tyrannies, and cruelties they were committing among those gentle, innocent peoples; how they could not be saved while holding the Indians in encomiendas, nor could the one who distributed them; the obligation to restitution by which they were bound; and that he, from understanding the danger in which he lived, had given up his Indians—and many other things on the subject.

All were astonished, and even frightened, at what he told them. Some were repentant, others behaved as if they were dreaming—hearing something so novel as a declaration that they could not, without being considered sinners, possess Indians. They did not believe it, as if it were said that they could not make use of the beasts of the field.

This was preached on that day and was repeated many times afterward in other sermons, when an occasion of speaking offered. But when he saw that that island was taking the road followed by this Hispaniola and would shortly be destroyed, and that such wickedness and tyranny ... could not be rooted out unless the king were informed, he decided to go to Castile, to report to the king what was happening, and to seek urgently a remedy for such evils. He decided to go in any way he could, although he did not possess a single maravedi, nor whence to have any, but only one mare which might be worth up to 100 gold pesos.

Settled in this purpose, he wrote Pedro de la Rentería, his true friend and partner in the estate, who, as I said, was in Jamaica, that he had decided to go to Castile on certain business of great importance. This was such, and so pressing, that unless Rentería hastened his coming he would leave without waiting for him, something the good Rentería could scarcely imagine.

And I will relate here a matter worthy of careful consideration. This is that when Rentería ... spent one entire Lent in a Franciscan monastery ... in that island of Jamaica, while his departure for the island of Cuba was being arranged ... , the thought of the oppression of those peoples and of the sad life they suffered came to him, and that it would be well to seek some remedy from the king ... , at least for the children (for he considered it impossible to remove everyone from the Spaniards' power. Hence he concluded that he ought to ask the king for authority to establish certain schools and to gather all the children there for religious instruction. ...

With this purpose in mind, he decided that after he returned to the island of Cuba he would go on to Castile and seek the said power from the king. Thus both partners ... determined to go to Castile to solicit a remedy from the king for the misfortunes of these peoples, without either knowing about the other, rather, while there were 200 leagues between them.

Having then received Father Casas' letter, Rentería hurried as fast as he could to leave the island of Jamaica for that of Cuba. He arrived a league or two from the port, where the governor and the father cleric happened to be, along with the rest of the people. As they saw the caravel coming, the cleric went immediately in a canoe to receive his Rentería. And after he climbed into the caravel and they embraced, like persons who loved each other well, Rentería said: "What was it you wrote me about going to Castile? I, not you, must go to Castile, for as soon as I tell you why I have decided to go you will rejoice. ..."

The cleric said: "Now then, let's go ashore, and soon as I

reveal to you my purpose in thinking of going to Castile, I know you will consider it good not to go yourself, but that I go."

They went ashore, and Rentería was received by the governor and greeted by everyone with much pleasure, because he was loved by all. When night arrived and they remained alone, they agreed that each would make known the reason . . . for his journey. And after a friendly contention over who would speak first, Rentería, who was very humble, conceded that he would tell his design beforehand.

"I," he said, "have sometimes thought of the miseries, afflictions, and evil life which these peoples endure, and how every day, here as in Hispaniola, they are all consumed and perish. It has seemed to me that it would be an act of compassion to go report this to the king, since he must know nothing of it, and to ask him to at least let us establish some schools in which the children might be brought up and taught, and where we might free them from so violent and fierce a death."

When the cleric heard his reason, he marveled and gave thanks to God. . . . He answered him: "Then know, señor and brother, that my purpose is no other than to go seek a total remedy for these unfortunates whom we see thus perishing. . . . For know that I have long studied and pondered this matter, from a certain day when I was to preach in such a place. And I find that neither the king nor any other power there may be on earth can justify our tyrannical entrance into these Indies, nor these infernal repartimientos by which we kill them and devastate these lands, as is seen in the islands of Hispaniola, San Juan, and Jamaica, and in all of the Lucayos.

The results, past and present, of our deeds condemn our tyranny and wickedness, since we have cast so many innocent peoples into hell without faith and without the sacraments, with such great destruction. Besides this, I have this reason and that one, and this authority and these others may be scrutinized. In sum, it is enough to say that all we do and have done is contrary to the intention of Jesus Christ, contrary to the method of charity which he recommended to us in his Gospel, and, if you consider it carefully, . . . contradicts all of the Holy Scripture.

"And know that I have preached this, and such and such has happened. And Diego Velázquez and many who have heard me are very surprised and somewhat repentant, especially seeing that I have given up my Indians, whence they judge that I have not stirred myself up for nothing."

When the good Rentería heard this, he was full of joy and wonder. He gave thanks to God, because it seemed to him that his kind impulse and great desire were also strengthened, and he spoke to the father as follows:

"Now I do say, father, that not I but you must go . . . to Castile and describe to the king all the wrongs and the ruin of these peoples here. And I say that you should ask for the necessary remedy, since, as an educated man, you will know better how to establish a foundation for what you say. For that purpose, take our estate and everything I bring in this caravel, and let as much money as possible be raised from them. And take the money, so that you can stay at court as long as necessary to assist these peoples. And may God our Lord be he who ever guides and protects you."

In the caravel he had brought many swine and much cassava bread . . . and maize, and other things worth a great deal. From this and from what else they had at hand, they raised some money, a good sum, which the father took so that he could remain at court for those years, as will appear below.

✤{ 11 }✤

First Battles at Court

The following selection, from Book III, Chapters 84 and 85, depicts the situation Las Casas faced when he returned to Spain in 1515 and encountered corrupt officials who profited from holding Indians in encomiendas yet were supposed to govern the Indies justly. The king's secretary, Lope Conchillos, and the bishop of Burgos, Juan Rodríguez de Fonseca, controlled Indian affairs. (Obras Escogidas, II, 367-371.)

The cleric arrived at Plasencia, where the Catholic king was at the time, a few days before Christmas in the same year, 1515. And as he knew that the bishop of Burgos and Secretary Conchillos held many Indians in all four of these islands — Hispaniola, Cuba, Jamaica, and San Juan — and thought they would oppose him, he did not care to speak to them but desired to arrange to talk with the king. He wished to give him the archbishop of Seville's letter and, besides, to inform him of his purpose in coming.

This took place, for one night, the evening before Christmas Eve, he spoke to the king at length and related his purpose in coming, which was to make known to him the destruction of these lands and the violent deaths of their native peoples; how the Spaniards, by their avarice, were killing them: how all were perishing without faith and without the sacraments; and that if His Highness did not assist shortly with a remedy, all the lands would soon become wilderness. He declared that . . . since this was a matter that meant much to the royal conscience and estate, and it was necessary to inform His Highness about it in great detail . . . , he begged that, when it pleased His Highness he would give him a long audience.

The king replied that it pleased him to grant that, and that he would hear him one day during that Christmas season. The cleric gave him the archbishop of Seville's letter, kissed his hands, and departed. The king then sent the letter to Secretary Conchillos; and I believe, without having seen it, that as it concerned the Indians and revealed the stratagem of what Father Casas was seeking, neither Conchillos nor the bishop of Burgos received much joy from it.

It is also thought that Diego Velázquez, suspecting that the said cleric could do him some damage by telling the king and likewise the Admiral, whose deputy Velázquez was, something of what was happening in that island, wrote the treasurer Pasamonte about the cleric's preaching against those who held Indians or favored the Admiral's affairs, and that the treasurer wrote Conchillos and the bishop of Burgos. . . .

Meanwhile, the cleric decided to speak to the king's confessor, a Dominican friar named Fray Tomás de Matienzo . . . and tell him something of the oppression, tyranny, and calamities the Indians suffered; also, to tell him of the opposition he feared from the bishop, Conchillos, and others on the Council who held many Indians and thus had so much at stake — although their Indians were the ones most cruelly treated. He declared that it was proper that that the king alone should understand this business first. . . .

The confessor spoke to the king, informing him of the wrongs and injustices committed in these islands, the decrease of the Indians because of the wrongs, and all the rest affirmed by the cleric. But since the king decided to depart for Seville on Holy Innocents' Day, the fourth day of the Christmas feast, he told the confessor there would be no occasion to hear the cleric there, but that the confessor, on his behalf, should tell the cleric to go to Seville. There the king would hear him at leisure and would provide a remedy for all those grievances and evils.

The confessor added that he thought the cleric should say something, chiefly to the bishop and Conchillos, and inform them of the wrongs suffered by those peoples, how these lands were becoming depopulated, and how necessary remedies were. For in the end this matter must come into their hands, and it would be well that they be notified and perhaps softened by his tale of the plaints of the Indians. The cleric, although against his will . . . . agreed to go sound them out.

He went first to Secretary Conchillos, who already knew, from the archbishop's letter to the king, why the cleric came. He received him very well and began to flatter him with pleasing words and to be reconciled with him to such a degree that the cleric might feel encouraged to request any honor or benefit he desired in these Indies, and Conchillos would give it to him. But divine mercy had considered it good to remove the cleric from the darkness in which all the others were perishing, and as was manifest afterward, God had chosen him . . . to explain and abhor that moral pestilence . . . , freeing him from all greed for any private temporal advantage. Therefore the flatteries of Conchillos and the expectations the cleric could have from them moved him little to abandon . . . the purpose which God had inspired in him.

He determined to speak to the bishop, in order to follow the judgment of the said confessor. And one night, after asking and being granted an audience with him, he reported, by a written memorial which he carried, some of the cruelties committed in his presence in the island of Cuba. Among them, he read an account of the death of 7,000 children in three months. . . . And when the cleric was aggrieved at the death of those innocents as a monstrous happening, the bishop replied (it was he who governed all these Indies): "Behold, what a witty fool! What is that to me, and what is that to the king?" — in these very words.

Then the cleric raises his voice and said: "What is it to your lordship and to the king that those souls die? Oh, great and eternal God! Who is there to whom that is something?" And saying this, he leaves. . . .

The cleric then went to Seville, as ordered, to await the king. . . . But just after the cleric arrived in Seville, through the wretched luck of these unhappy Indian peoples and also because of the demerits and sins of Spain, there came a message that the Catholic king had passed from this world to the other. Great was the grief and anguish which the cleric received from the death of the king. For, because of the king's being old, very near death, and disengaged from wars, a great hope had been born in the cleric that when the king learned the truth from him, the Indies would be relieved. ... For the cleric often said that to assist the Indies naught was needed but a king who was old, with one foot in the grave, and free of wars.

Finally, he recovered his spirits and decided to go to Flanders to inform the prince Don Carlos and seek a remedy for such great wrongs from him, as from the one who was succeeding to the kingdoms there and here.

Las Casas tells how in Madrid Cardinal Cisneros asked him to remain in Spain and promised to help the Indians. Las Casas then describes, below, one of the conferences on Indian affairs arranged by the cardinal.

One day, the cardinal Adrian and the others being present at the ... meeting, it happened that the cardinal ordered the laws made in Burgos in 1512 to be read. ... He did this on account of the cleric's complaints that the laws were unjust because of the deception practiced on the Catholic king and on the king's council by those who held Indians here. (However, the council had been more credulous than it should have been, and perhaps some of the members wished consciously to be deceived because of the profit they were hoping for and later had.)

A servant and official of Secretary Conchillos read the laws. And when he arrived, I believe, the law ordering Indians who worked on estates or farms to be given a pound of meat every eight days or on feast days, he wanted to conceal that, perhaps because it affected him or his friends, and he read it in a different way from the way it was written. But the cleric, who had studied it carefully and knew it by heart, said at once there in the presence of all: "That law doesn't say any such thing."

The cardinal ordered the reader to go back and read it again. He read it in the same way, The cleric said: "That law doesn't say any such thing."

The cardinal, as if angry at the cleric and supporting the

reader, said: "Be quiet, or consider what you are saying."

The cleric replied: "May your most reverend lordship order my head struck off if what notary so-and-so recites is truly what that law says."

Then they take the laws from the official's hand and discover what the cleric had declared. It may well be believed that so-and-so (for the sake of his honor I don't want to name him) perhaps wished never to have been born in order not to experience the shame he experienced there.

⛤{ 12 }⛤

Black Slaves in the New World

The following selection, from Book III, Chapter 129, relates how Las Casas in 1518 passed on a suggestion that a few Black slaves from Spain be used to help some colonists set up sugar mills and free their Indians, and his later repentance for making the proposal. Although similar suggestions were being made at the time by many others — Jeronymite commissioners, friars, and court officials — the large-scale introduction of Black slaves from Africa began a decade and a half later after the total extermination of the Indians of the greater and lesser Antilles and along the Caribbean coasts. (Obras Escogidas, II, 487-488.)

Before sugar mills were invented, certain inhabitants who retained something of what they had acquired by the sweat and blood of the Indians, desired permission to send to Castile to buy some Negro slaves, as they saw that the Indians were becoming fewer. There were even some ... who promised the cleric Bartolomé de las Casas that if he brought, or gained permission to bring, a dozen Negroes to this island, they would give up their Indians so these Indians could be set free.

When the said cleric understood this — and as he enjoyed great favor after the king came to Spain to rule, and as the remedies for those lands were placed in his hands — he secured this from the king: that in order to free the Indians the Spaniards of these islands would be allowed to take some Negro slaves from Castile.

The council decided ... that permission should be given to take 4,000, for the time being, for the four islands—this Hispaniola, and the islands of San Juan, Cuba, and Jamaica. When it was known that permission had been granted, not one of the Spaniards from these Indies who were then at court failed to counsel the governor of Bresa, a Flemish gentleman who had come with the king and was a great favorite, to ask for that privilege. He requested it, and it was bestowed immediately. Then he sold it for 25,000 ducats to the Genoese, under a thousand conditions which they knew how to demand; and one condition was that for eight years no license could be granted to anyone else to bring Negro slaves to the Indies.

Afterward, the Genoese sold each license for at least eight ducats per Negro. Thus, what the cleric de las Casas had secured in order that the Spaniards could be helped ... to maintain themselves on the land, so they would leave the Indians at liberty, was made salable to merchants, which was no small hindrance to the welfare and liberation of the Indians.

Not long afterward, the cleric found himself regretting this counsel he had given, and judged himself guilty through carelessness. For since he later observed and found out ... that the Negroes' captivity was as unjust as the Indians', the remedy he had recommended—to bring Negroes in order to free the Indians—was not a prudent one, although he then supposed that the Negroes had been made captives justly. However, it was not certain that his ignorance and good intention in this would excuse him before the divine judgment.

There were then in this island of Hispaniola as many as ten or twelve of the king's Negroes who had been brought to build the fort above and at the mouth of the river. But after this license was given and that fort finished, many other licenses followed, so that over 30,000 Negroes have been brought to this island and more than 100,000, as I believe, to all the Indies. And never for that were the Indians assisted or freed, since the cleric Casas could not pursue the matter, the king being absent and the council members new each day and ignorant of the [natural and divine] law they should have known. ... And as the sugar mills increased every day, the need to place Negroes in them increased, for each sugar mill using water requires at least eighty Negroes, and the sugar-mills using horses, thirty or forty. . . .

Hence it resulted that when the Portuguese, who for many years have had a vocation to plunder Guinea and unjustly enslave Negroes, saw our need and how we were buying slaves at a great rate, they hastened — and hasten every day — to abduct and capture them in as many wicked ways as they can. Likewise, since the Negroes themselves see that the Portuguese desire and seek them so eagerly, they wage unjust wars among themselves and in other illicit ways steal and sell each other to the Portuguese. Thus we are the cause of all the sins which they commit against each other, as well as our own in buying them.

❧{ 13 }❧

Las Casas Joins the Dominicans

The following selection from Book III, Chapters 159 and 160, tells how Las Casas learned early in 1522 of the Indian uprising that ended his attempt to found a colony in Venezuela (see pp. 6-8), and how he then entered the Dominican Order. (Obras Escogidas, II, 563, 566-567.)

The said cleric came from Yaguana [in western Hispaniola] toward this city of Santo Domingo, accompanied by certain persons, and while they were taking a nap by a river, he being asleep under a tree, some travelers arrived there. When they were asked by the persons already there what news they had of the city or of Castile, they replied: "Only that the Indians of the Pearl Coast have slain the cleric Bartolomé de las Casas and all his household."

The ones there replied: "We ourselves are witnesses that that is impossible."

While they were wrangling over that, the cleric awoke as if from an abyss, and when he understood the news he did not know what to say nor whether to believe it. But considering the condition of the land when he left it and the events that had occurred, he began to fear and believe that all his labor must be lost.

And as he learned more about these matters afterward, he thought it was a divine judgment, punishing and afflicting him for entering into partnership with those who, in his opinion, did not help or favor for love of God, nor out of zeal to win the souls perishing throughout those provinces, but only because of avarice to become rich. And it appears that he offended God by staining the purity of his spiritual affairs . . . with the filth and earthly impurity of such human, even inhuman, means, so incommensurate with those adopted by Jesus Christ. . . .

To this the cleric replied that if he made such haste to accept the terms offered him by the Audiencia, he did so to hinder the injuries and deaths the fleet was causing, and this reason appears sufficient. He could be answered, it seems, that he was not obligated to go that far, etc. In brief, it may piously be believed that Our Lord considered his good intention and not his deed . . . , and therefore freed him from that death which he would have suffered with the others. However—with divine assistance—if he had been there in Cumaná, the ships would not have withdrawn, nor is it to be believed that he would have been negligent in so great a danger, during the three days when the plot was known.

Finally, after hearing this sad news, he continued his journey toward this city of Santo Domingo, grieving and anxious to learn fully what had happened.

To conclude the history of the father cleric: when he arrived at Santo Domingo he wrote the king about everything that was happening and then decided to wait for a reply because he did not have the means to go to court in person—although there would have been someone to assist and lend him money if he wished to go. And certainly if he had gone . . . , he would have arrived when the king had finally returned to those kingdoms of Castile and Aragon along with the gentlemen and favorites who had helped the cleric. . . .

As soon as those very individuals learned what had taken place, they wrote him that he should return, that he would have more favor with the king than before; and Pope Adrian himself also ordered him to write. But the letters came when he could no longer decide for himself. Perhaps if, after reaching this city of Santo Domingo, he had then left for Castile . . . , the tyranny in these Indies would have been driven out.

But truly God did not put it in his heart to go, either because he did not deserve it or because, in accord with the profound divine judgment, those peoples along with so many others had to be lost, or, besides, because the atrocious sins committed by our race against those peoples were not to be so quickly ended.

Therefore, after he had written the king what was most suitable, he awaited the reply for some months. And meanwhile his conversation was commonly with the Dominicans, especially with a father named Fray Domingo de Betanzos, a religious of outstanding virtue and devotion. This father pressed him often to become a friar, saying that he had labored enough for the Indians and that now that so pious a business had collapsed, it appeared that God did not wish to make use of him in this way.

Among other answers and excuses the cleric gave, one was to say that it was proper to await the king's reply to see what he commanded. The good father answered: "Tell me, father, if you die in the meantime, who will receive the king's command or his letters?" These words pierced the cleric Casas' soul, and from then on he began to think more frequently about his condition. And in the end, he decided to reckon that he was already dead when the king's letters or replies should arrive.

So he asked for the habit urgently, and they gave it to him, with great gladness on the part of the friars and with no less on the part of the whole city and all the Indies, as soon as they knew, although friars and laymen rejoiced in different ways and for different reasons.

For the friars rejoiced spiritually, because of the benefit of the conversion of one they dearly loved; and the laymen rejoiced because they realized that that one who hindered the robberies they carried out and intended to carry out . . . would be missing, as if they saw him buried. Except that afterward, in spite of many, he revived, one may believe by God's will, to hinder certain evils that he hindered with divine assistance and to point out to the world with his finger, like the sun, the dangerous state in which many were living. . . .

During his novitiate, letters came from Cardinal Adrian, who was Pope, and from the Flemish gentlemen, urging him to return to court and stating that he would enjoy as much favor as they had given him the other time, and more. And the superiors of the monastery did not wish to show him the letters, perhaps lest he become uneasy. . . .

And with this, let us cease to discuss the affairs of the cleric, now a friar, Fray Bartolomé de las Casas for some years, during which he, to all appearances, slept; until the time comes, if God grant us life, when we shall return to his history, of which there will be much to say.

PART III

ANTHROPOLOGIST

THE APOLOGETIC HISTORY

In 1527, while living in a Dominican monastery in Puerto de Plata, Hispaniola, Las Casas began to write his chronicle, the *History of the Indies*. In his Prologue to this work, written in 1552 in Spain, he says he planned to include something about the "quality, nature, and properties of these regions" of the Indies, and also about the "customs, religion, rites, ceremonies, and condition of the native peoples."[1]

Las Casas did describe the "quality, nature, and properties of these regions" in the first twenty-two chapters of what is now his *Apologetic History*. These were apparently written early and placed after Chapter 67 of Book I of the *History of the Indies*. At some point, however, Las Casas realized that his digression on geography and customs was becoming too lengthy to be included in the *History of the Indies*. By then he had written more chapters and supplied an Aristotelian framework for this material, perhaps to combat those who used Aristotle to prove that the Indians were "slaves by nature"; now he detached the chapters he had finished — more than a hundred — and made them the first part of a new work, which he completed probably in the 1550s. He titled it the *Apologetic History* (or "Defensive Account") and according to some scholars may have used it, or a prototype of it, in his debate with Sepúlveda in 1550-1551. It was not printed in full until 1909.

This chronology and possible collection of the *Apologetic History* with the Sepúlveda controversy have been sharply challenged by Edmundo O'Gorman. O'Gorman argues, on the basis of inferences from a close reading of the Las Casas texts, that the *Apologetic History* was not conceived until after 1552 — *after* the debate with Sepúlveda and as a result of Las Casas' alleged loss of that debate. It was composed between 1555 and 1559, in

Spain, the early chapters from the *History of the Indies* being
transferred only then. In O'Gorman's opinion, the *Apologetic
History*, and not the unfinished *History of the Indies*, is Las Casas'
masterpiece.[2]

Although the *Apologetic History* has been called a "book
sealed with seven seals, which no one had the curiosity to break
or the patience to read,"[3] running through its "welter of fact
and fantasy"[4] is a logically developed argument. The 1,350-page
work is a comparison, using criteria from Aristotle's *Politics*, of
the culture of "these Indian peoples" of the New World to that
of famous nations of the Old. Its thesis is that the Indian is not
a "slave by nature," but is eminently rational. He is the equal,
or in some things the superior, of the ancient Greeks, Romans,
Egyptians, Spaniards, etc.; therefore his human dignity and
capacity for good should be respected.

The *Apologetic History* may be outlined as follows:[5]

    I. Argument: preamble—purpose and brief outline of
       contents

   II. Chapters 1-22: the physical environment—abundant
       resources of Hispaniola, typical of all the Indies

  III. Chapters 23-39: six natural causes of a good under-
       standing—influence of stars, body make-up, climate,
       etc.

  IV. Chapters 40-58: Aristotelian standards for civil life—
       three kinds of prudence, six classes of citizens, the
       existence of cities

   V. Chapters 59-60: first class of citizens—farmers

  VI. Chapters 61-65: second class of citizens—craftsmen

 VII. Chapters 66-68: third class of citizens—warriors

VIII. Chapters 69-70: fourth class of citizens—men of
       wealth

  IX. Chapters 71-194: fifth class of citizens—priests

   X. Chapters 195-262: sixth class of citizens—judges and
       governors

  XI. Chapter 263: conclusion—equality or superiority of
       Indians to peoples of the Old World

 XII. Chapters 264-267 and Epilogue: epilogue—four dif-
       ferent meanings of "barbarous"

As this schema shows, Las Casas devoted most of his attention
to the religious and political life of the Indians (IX, X) and

found the best evidence for their rationality therein.

What place does the *Apologetic History* occupy in the history of ideas? According to Lewis Hanke, Las Casas' insistence that the Indians had a civilization of their own, worthy of study and respect, foreshadowed the comparative study of cultures, and the anthropologist's scientific approach to primitive peoples.[6] Las Casas did not condemn the Indian way of life because it was different from the European; he explained and defended it, even while retaining his classical-Christian standards.

As Pérez de Tudela points out, Las Casas was able to press his defense to the limit and to give Europe the concept of the "Noble Savage" because his Indian ("these Indian peoples") was an abstraction, a mosaic of the good qualities of the diverse inhabitants of the New World.[7] As much as possible, Las Casas dismissed the Indians' defects as accidents; the favorable characteristics were the substance. (The conquistadors did just the opposite: they abstracted the Indian's bad qualities and presented them as a complete picture of a creature who was bestial and a "slave by nature.") Las Casas emphasized the Indian's rationality, as shown in his domestic, religious, and political life — above all, his potentiality to rise in the scale of civilization and to assimilate Christian values. Las Casas' anthropology, says Pérez de Tudela, is an "anthropology of hope."[8]

Las Casas thus occupies an intermediate position between St. Thomas Aquinas and Jean Jacques Rousseau. For Aquinas, natural man was an unalterable substance, which not even the Redemption could change. For Las Casas, however, natural man, who seemed to be typified by the Indian, was more of an entity in transition — a voyager on the sea of history. What was important about him was not so much his substance, which was tainted with original sin — this separates Las Casas from Rousseau — as his promise of future good. Enraptured by the simple, appealing virtues of the primitive peoples, Las Casas looked beyond scholasticism toward the idea of progress — an ascent of humanity through the ages.

NOTES

1. Bartolomé de Las Casas, *Obras Escogidas*, ed. Juan Pérez de Tudela (Madrid: Biblioteca de Autores Españoles, 1957-1958), I, 16-17.

2. Edmundo O'Gorman, "Estudio Preliminar," especially pp. xvii, xxxv, lvii, and lviii, in Bartolomé de Las Casas, *Apologética historia sumaria*, ed. O'Gorman (Mexico City: Universidad Nacional Autónoma, 1967), I, xv ff.

3. Manuel Serrano y Sanz, "Doctrinas psicológicas de Fr. Bartolomé de Las Casas," *Revista de archivos, bibliotecas, y museos*, 17 (Madrid 1907), 59-60, as quoted in Lewis Hanke, *Bartolomé de Las Casas* (The Hague: Martinus Nijhoff, 1951), p. 66.

4. Hanke, *Bartolomé de Las Casas*, p. 74.

5. Based on Edmundo O'Gorman's analysis in his "Estudio Preliminar," pp. xxxvi-lv.

6. Hanke, *Bartolomé de Las Casas*, pp. 88-89.

7. Juan Pérez de Tudela, "Estudio Crítico Preliminar," in Bartolomé de Las Casas, *Obras Escogidas,* ed. Pérez de Tudela (Madrid: Biblioteca de Autores Españoles, 1957), I, cxvii.

8. Ibid.

❧{ 14 }❧

The Rationality of the American Indian

The following selection, from the Argument at the beginning of the Apologetic History, *states Las Casas' thesis and plan for the work.* (Obras Escogidas, *III, 3-4.*)

The final cause of writing this *Apologetic History* was the author's observation that all the infinite races of that immense world had been defamed by certain persons . . . who proclaimed that these were not peoples possessing sound reason by which to govern themselves; that they lacked well-ordered republics and a human way of life. They proclaimed this simply because they found these peoples so gentle, patient, and humble, as if Divine Providence had been negligent in the creation of innumerable rational souls and had allowed human nature to go astray . . . so that the Indians all proved unsocial and thus monstrous. . . .

To demonstrate the truth, which is the opposite (after a description including the qualities and blessedness, the geography and something of the cosmography of these lands), six natural causes of rationality in the Indians are collected and compiled in this book. These six natural causes . . . are: the influence of the stars; the condition of the lands; the makeup of

From Bartolomé de Las Casas, *Obras Escogidas*, 5 vols., ed. Juan Pérez de Tudela (Madrid: Biblioteca de Autores Españoles, 1957-1958).

the parts and organs of the exterior and interior senses; the mildness of the climate; the age of the fathers when the children are born; and the excellence and wholesomeness of the food. . . .

Four other accidental causes of rationality . . . are their temperance in eating and drinking; their moderation in love-making: their lack of anxiety and care about worldly things; and also their not being disturbed by the passions of the soul, that is, by anger, joy, love, etc.

From all these causes . . . it is proved and concluded, and evidence is given, that these peoples . . . to a greater or less degree, but with none completely destitute in this respect, have excellent, subtle and very capable minds. They are likewise prudent, and endowed by nature with the three kinds of prudence named by the Philosopher [Aristotle]: monastic, economic, and political. Political prudence includes the six parts which, according to Aristotle, make any republic self-sufficient and prosperous: farmers; craftsmen; warriors; men of wealth; priests (who understand religion, sacrifices, and everything pertaining to divine worship); and sixth, judges or ministers of justice or men who govern well. . . .

As for political prudence, I say that not only have the Indians shown themselves to be very prudent peoples, with acute minds, having justly and prosperously governed their republics (so far as they could without faith and the knowledge of the true God), but they have equalled many diverse races of the past and present, much praised for government, way of life, and customs. And in following the rules of natural reason, they have even surpassed by not a little those who were the most prudent of all, such as the Greeks and Romans. This advantage . . . will appear very clearly, if it please God, when the Indian races are compared with others.

❧{ 15 }❧

A Description of Cuba

The following selection, from Book III, Chapter 22 of the History of the Indies, *contains descriptive material similar to that found in earlier chapters of the* History of the Indies *that were transferred to the* Apologetic History. *Las Casas lived in Cuba from 1513 to 1515. (*Obras Escogidas, *II, 225-228.)*

The island of Cuba is a little less than 300 leagues long, measured by land, although by air or by water there are not that many leagues. Beginning with the cape or point farthest east, called Cape Maisi, for almost a third of its length it is fifty-five or sixty leagues wide; then it begins to narrow and continues narrowing to the last cape or western point, which is about twenty leagues across. Its location is within the Tropic of Cancer, in 20, 20 1/2, and up to 21 degrees [north latitude].

Nearly all the land is level, and all full of forests. From the eastern point of Maisi, for thirty leagues or more, it has very high ridges, and likewise in the west after two-thirds of it has been passed, while there are others in the middle of the island, although not very high. Delightful rivers flow from one part toward the north and from another toward the south; they are full of fish, especially mullet and shad, which enter and ascend the rivers from the sea.

Almost halfway along the island, off the southern coast, there are an infinite number of clustered islets which . . . the Admiral

[Christopher Columbus] called the Garden of the Queen, when he discovered them on his second voyage. There are other islets, although not so many, off the northern coast; Diego Velázquez named these the Garden of the King. A powerful river, called Cauto by the Indians, pours forth in about the middle of the southern coast—a river with very beautiful banks where breed an infinite number of crocodiles, which we mistakenly call lizards. ... Many rivers and streams contained a great deal of gold. ...

As I said, the island of Cuba is very heavily wooded, so that one can walk nearly 300 leagues under the trees. These are of many kinds, like those in this Hispaniola, and among others there are very handsome cedars, fragrant and red-colored, and as thick as stout oxen. From these, the Indians made the large canoes which held fifty to seventy men, to voyage on the sea; and Cuba was very rich in them in its time. There are other, sweetgum trees. We are not well acquainted with them, but if we station ourselves on some high ground in the mornings, it is marvelous how sweet a scent is perceived ... because the precious sweet gum is burnt and is sensed in the mists of the earth, ascending, at sunrise, from fires the Indians made at night. For they always have a fire at night, not because it is cold—but it is cool for them, not having beds like us but only some hammocks.

There are some trees which produce a fruit called *xaguas,* the first syllable long, as large as veal kidneys. When these are picked from the tree, even though they are not ripe, and left in a corner of the house for three or four days to ripen, they all fill with honey; and everything inside, which is a certain meat— or I don't know what to compare it to—is not less delicious, and I can say more delicious, than a candied pear.

Throughout the island of Cuba there are so many wild vines with grapes on them that there are places where, within the circle of one crossbow shot, 100 or 200 loads of grapes could be gathered. And wine could be made from the grapes, although it would be sour; but I myself drank some that was not so sour. Thus if the grapes were cultivated and given sun and wind, doubtless they would become domesticated and sweet. But since they grow in the forests and among large trees, the sun does not warm them nor does the air cool them. ... Many vines which we saw were much thicker than a man, and it is no exaggeration to say this. And this is no wonder, since the cedars and other trees are so thick, as we said above, owing to the great moisture and fertility of the island. All of it is fresher and more temperate than this island of Hispaniola; it is a very healthful land.

Cuba has excellent ports, much more sheltered and secure for many ships than if they had been hand-made, especially along the southern coast. Such is the port of the city of Santiago, which is in the form of a cross; but I don't believe there could be a better port than that of Xagua, and perhaps not its equal in the whole world. . . .

The ships enter through a strait, which is about a crossbow shot wide, or a little more, if I have not forgotten, and within the port there are ten leagues of water, with three islets. At one or two of these islets one can make ships fast to a stanchion so that they don't stir from there because that entire roomy harbor is enclosed by ridges; it is as if one were inside a house.

There are so many fish in this port, especially mullet, that the Indians had pens made of canes sunk into the sea itself. Within these pens, twenty, thirty, or fifty thousand mullet were enclosed and partitioned off so that not one could get out. The Indians would take as many as they wanted from the pen with their nets and leave the others, just as if they were in a reservoir or tank.

On the north coast there are also good ports. The best, and a very good one, is the one they call Carenas, now Havana. This is excellent, able to hold many ships; there are few in Spain, and perhaps in many other parts of the world, which equal it. It is almost at the end of the island, toward the west; and twenty leagues from there, to the east, there is another, called Matanzas, but it is not very safe or protected. The port which they call Príncipe is also very good, and this is nearly in the middle of the island; almost at the eastern end is another called Baracoa, a fair port, and there are some others between Baracoa and Príncipe which provide good anchorages for ships.

There are many birds in that island, such as doves and turtledoves and natural partridges like those in Spain, but smaller, and except for the breast they have little meat. . . . Cranes are found only in Cuba and Tierra Firme. . . . There is a multitude of very pleasing parrots, quite green except that above their bills, on their foreheads, they have a tiny patch of red feathers; in this they differ from the parrots of Hispaniola, because those are white, or almost plucked, above the bill. Throughout May and from then on, when they are young, they are much better to eat, boiled or roasted, than thrush in season, or other good birds.

The Indians caught as many as they wished, without one escaping, in this way. A boy ten or fifteen years old would climb into a tree with a live parrot. He would place a bit of grass or straw over his head, and then hit the parrot on the head with his hand. The parrot would cry out as if complaining.

Immediately, countless parrots in the air, hearing the captive parrot, all come and alight on the tree. The boy has a slender stick with a thin cord looped at the end. Very slowly, so that the parrot does not become frightened by the stick but thinks it a part of the tree itself, the boy drops the loop around the neck of each parrot. Now he draws the parrot near at hand. He wrings the parrot's neck, and drops it below, and does thus to all he wishes until he sees the ground below covered with parrots. . . .

There were wonderful snakes in that island, as thick as the stout leg of a man, and quite large, all of them brown. They were very sluggish, so that a man would tread on them when they were coiled, and they scarcely perceived it. There were also iguanas, which are properly serpents; these are shaped like lizards, are colored, and are as large as lap-dogs. They are better than pheasants for eating, our Spaniards say, but they could never prove it by me.

That island is almost too rich in fish. Along both coasts there is an abundance of mullet, sea-fish like those of Castile, very large shad, needlefish, and many others. But along the southern coast, where there are an infinite number of islets called the Garden of the Queen, as I said, and the sea is stagnant between these and the large island of Cuba, there breed so many turtles that they are without number, and fishing for them is excellent. The turtles are as large as a large buckler, or even a shield. Each one . . . usually weighs 100 pounds.

Turtle is very good to eat, and quite healthful. Its fat is like the fat of a hen, so yellow and it seems molten like gold. It is good for clearing up leprosy, itch, and similar diseases. Ten men and more can stuff themselves eating one turtle. The turtle has 500 or 600 eggs, like hens; but the eggs do not have shells, rather they have a thin membrane. Turtles leave the sea to deposit their eggs on land and bury them in the sand. Then the sun with the sand hatches them; a little turtle crawls out of each egg, and immediately all go to seek the sea by natural instinct.

This is the method of fishing for them. The Indians would take a fish which mariners call a "reverse fish" [suckerfish or remora] as large as a good thick sardine, attach a thin cord thirty to fifty fathoms long to its tail, and cast the fish into the sea. The little fish then goes to look for turtles, and after it found them would stick beneath the shell of one.

When the Indian saw that it was time, he would pull his cord in bit by bit and draw the 100-pound turtle through the water as if he were drawing a small gourd. The little remora, after fastening itself wherever it does, can never be detached from the turtle unless the remora is broken to pieces. In this way, the Indians caught so many turtles that each time as much meat could have been butchered, and was, as could be had from 100 cows. And it has happened that 300 or 400 Indians would come to us laden with that meat or fish, which they presented to us. For just as we said that they had pens for mullet, so also, between those islets, they had pens of 500 or 1,000 turtles, so that not one was able to escape from these enclosures, consisting of a fence of canes.

Furthermore, as for cassava bread, we found that island full of those plantings. And never was there a land discovered in these Indies which, in the abundance of food and of necessary things, would surpass Cuba.

❈{ 16 }❈

The Ill Effects of Sadness and Fear

The following selection, from Chapters 28 and 37 of the Apologetic History, *discusses bodily changes caused by certain emotions. It is part of Las Casas' treatment of the six natural causes influencing the rationality of the Indians — specifically, the make-up of the body and the presence or absence of the "common passions."* (Obras Escogidas, *III, 88-89, 124-125.*)

Sadness not less but more than joy, although not with such sudden and unexpected danger, causes a great change that is full of anguish. If the sadness is for some future evil, properly called loathing or vexation, it causes insomnia; if it is for past evil, it causes dreams; if it is for present evil, it oppresses and grieves the spirit, monopolizing every thought so that the spirit cannot free itself for intellectual work. Thus, St. Gregory says that because of sadness he stopped pursuing his exposition of Ezekiel after three chapters, leaving the others and passing on to explain the fortieth.

If the sadness and the evil which causes it increase so greatly that they completely take away the hope of escape, this altogether inhibits the interior operations of the anguished person's spirit. He does not know in which direction to turn, because he does not see where he will be able to breathe or be consoled. Thus, also, the exterior bodily operations are sometimes hindered, so that the man remains as though struck dumb, without feeling. So it is impossible for the sad person, with interior and exterior senses deadened, to lift up his spirit for intellectual accomplishments. And among all the passions of the soul, it is sadness which does the most damage to the health of the body....

Hence it is that excessive sadness, especially when joined to the fear arising from the imagination of a dreaded evil, according to the Philosopher [Aristotle], *Rhetoric*, Book II, Chapter 2, often causes pestilence. For a vivid imagination is so powerful that if a man imagines certain diseases, he brings them upon himself; if I imagine some pain my neighbor has, I will suffer that same pain. The reason is that man's body, and that of the higher animals, is naturally subject to the imagination as much as to changes produced by heat and cold.... For there naturally spring from the imagination the passions of the soul, which are joy, sorrow, hate, and love, and the others by which the heart is moved. If these spirits are disturbed, the entire body is altered.

Likewise, the entire body naturally obeys the imagination, if it is strong, in respect to falling from a high place. Thus if a man or an animal is in a high tower from which he can fall and imagine that he falls, he will not be able to keep from falling without realizing what he is doing.

The ... passions of the soul which can cause confusion and accidentally impede the acts of the understanding are grief, fear, sadness, anger, and rancor. From what has been demonstrated about the mildness of the Indians and the gentle quality of their society, it is evident that the last two passions do not prevail among them. As for the others, it must be assumed, from what can be gathered about the character of these peoples, that for the most part the Indians are by nature of a sanguine temperament, which is the noblest of the four temperaments. For its properties ... are very favorable to soul and body, and, for the most part, naturally cause virtuous inclinations in men.

One thing common to all sanguine persons, according to Albert [Albertus Magnus], is that they are cheerful, and that sadness cannot last long in them. They are gentle, benign, and affectionate in speech. They always have a sunny countenance. They are disposed to love, and easily form friendships with others. They are merry and cause laughter. They are merciful, open,

and generous, fit for all the arts, and for other good and praise-
worthy conditions and inclinations.

What has already been reported ... and what will now be
said bear witness that for the most part the Indians are sanguine.
All these peoples are very happy, from childhood on; they are
friends of music-making, dancing, and singing unaccompanied
when they lack instruments. They did have certain instruments
with which they made sounds or dancing and stirred themselves
to joy and gaiety. ... They are good and kind in a grand style,
which they exhibit when they receive guests and also at their
departure. The first Admiral [Christopher Columbus] who discovered this land was a reliable witness to this virtue.

In New Spain, when a guest visits them, they receive him
thus: "You have come to your own country and to your own
house. You may remain in it — you need lack for nothing." And
if it is an important person: "We are your vassals and servants —
you may, indeed, command us." There are similar words at
departure: "Watch where you are going — don't fall. Go one step
at a time so you don't stumble." ...

One sure and precise sign of this sanguine temperament in
the Indians is their patience and endurance in the intolerable
labors which they have suffered under the Spaniards, such hardships, and so numerous, as were never before imagined. ... This
is very clear from our daily experience among them. For while
doing work in the mines which would be unbearable not only
for men of flesh but also if the Indians were made of steel, and
even when carrying loads of three or four arrobas [an *arroba*
equals 25 pounds] on their shoulders, for fifty or a hundred
leagues on the highway, they go singing and laughing among
themselves, uttering a thousand of the jests that they have, as if
they were going along those roads to a feast.

Thus it seems that grief and sadness have less effect on them
than these passions would have on other races, all else being
equal, because of their noble, sanguine disposition and natural
gaiety. I have sometimes seen them stand pain and divers terrible torments with such patience that, although they were weeping and giving anguished, mournful cries, the pain and affliction
clearly appeared to exceed their perception of it.

Fear, however, joined to the sadness of an unhappy life and

their harsh and long-lasting slavery . . . produces stronger effects in these peoples that it could cause in others. This is so for four reasons. First, because of the magnitude and cruelty of their injuries, afflictions, labors, and continuing persecutions, which have crushed all their natural cheerfulness and noble temperament. Second, because of the long duration of the oppression, which they observe, so that many have lost hope of ever escaping, have despaired, and have died by their own hands from hanging or poison; this has completely banished their endurance and patience.

Third, because of the delicacy of their bodies and limbs, and because of their noble temperament, which causes anything injurious to be more painful to them than to others; therefore, they can stand less hardship and misfortune than other races — we see by experience how suddenly so many millions of them have perished, and how every day they are consumed. Fourth, because of the strength and power of their imagination which is more vivid than that of others.

❧{ 17 }❧

Indian Houses, Featherwork, and Silverwork

The following selection, from Chapters 43, 62, and 63 of the Apologetic History, *presents proof that the Indians possess (1) economic prudence (they build well-constructed houses for their families) and (2) effective members of one of the six classes of citizens required in a well-ordered republic — the craftsmen (they produce excellent featherwork and silver products).* (Obras Escogidas, *III, 146-147, 206-209.*)

If we would consider . . . the unmistakable evidence offered by communities large and small, living in peace, order, and concord, we must recognize clearly that the Indians . . . have had, and continue to have, this second kind of prudence, the domestic, in the government of their homes and families. But let us apply to them the specific rules and requirements of the Philosopher [Aristotle].

The first thing he says is incumbent upon men, in order that philosophers may be kings, is that they construct their own houses. These people built these houses in accord with the region they inhabited and their experience of their needs; they made them strong, suitable, and also attractive — very well fabricated. The inhabitants of this island of Hispaniola, of these neighboring islands, of the part of Tierra Firme near the shores of Paria, and elsewhere made their houses of wood and thatch in the shape of a bell. These were quite high and roomy, so that ten or more citizens with their families dwelt in each one.

They drove posts as a thick as a man's leg or thigh almost three feet deep into the ground, close together. All met overhead and were tied by lashings of woody vines. . . . Above this frame they placed many other thin pieces of wood crosswise, closely fastened with those vines. For the inside they made designs and symbols and patterns from wood and bark dyed black, and from other wood peeled so as to remain white so that they seemed to be made from some other beautiful painted materials.

They adorned other houses with reeds, peeled and very white — a kind of thin, delicate cane. They made very graceful ornaments and designs from these so that the interiors of the houses seemed to have been painted. Outside, they covered the houses with beautiful, fragrant grass. . . . I saw one of these Indian houses that a Spaniard sold to another for 600 castellanos or gold pesos, each one worth 450 maravedis.

In New Spain and for more than 500 leagues around Mexico City, they made houses of adobe or sun-baked brick, of wood, and many hewn stones — also in Florida and Cibola. In Peru, they made them of great hewn stones, almost like strong forts.

But what appears without double to exceed all human genius . . . is the art which those Mexican peoples have so perfectly mastered, of making from natural feathers, fixed in position with their own natural colors, anything that they or any other first-class painters can paint with brushes. They were accustomed to make many things out of feathers, such as animals, birds, men, capes or blankets to cover themselves, vestments for their priests, crowns or mitres, shields, flies, and a thousand other sorts of objects which they fancy.

These feathers were green, red or gold, purple, bright red, yellow, blue or pale green, black, white, and all the other colors, blended and pure, not dyed by human ingenuity but all natural, taken from various birds. Therefore they placed a high value on every species of birds, because they made use of all. They preserved the color hues of even the smallest birds that could be found on land or in the air, so that certain hues would harmonize with others, and they might adorn their work as much as, and more fittingly than, any painter in the world.

They would seat this feather on cotton cloth, or on a board, and on that would add little feathers of all colors, which they kept in small individual boxes or vessels, just as they would have taken prepared paints from shells or small saucers with paint brushes. If they wished to make a man's face, the form of an animal, or some other object which they had decided on and for which a white feather was needed, they selected one from the whites; if a green was required, they took one from the greens; if a red, from the reds; and they attached it very delicately, with a certain paste. Thus for the eyes in the face of a man or animal, requiring black and white and the pupil, they made, and continue to make, the different parts of feathers, with the delicacy of a great painter using a very fine brush—and surely this is a marvel.

And granted that before we Christians entered there they made perfect and wonderful things by this art, such as a tree, a rose, grass, a flower, an animal, a man, a bird, a dainty butterfly, a forest and a stone or rock, so skillfully that the object appeared alive or natural . . . , yet after the Spaniards went there and they saw our statues and other things, they had, beyond comparison, abundant material and an excellent opportunity to show the liveliness of their intellects, the integrity and disengagement of their powers or interior and exterior senses, and their great talent. For since our statues and altar-pieces are large and painted in divers colors, they had occasion to branch out, to practice, and to distinguish themselves in that new and delicate art of theirs, seeking to imitate our objects.

One of the great beauties they achieve in what they make— a canopy, cloak, vestment, or anything else especially large—is to place the feather in such a way that seen from one direction it appears gilded, although it lacks gold; from another, it seems iridescent; from another, it has a green luster, without being chiefly green; from another, viewed crossways, it has still another beautiful tint . . . and similarly from many other angles, all lustrous colors of marvelous attractiveness. Hence it is that one of their craftsmen is accustomed to go without food and drink for a whole day, arranging and removing feathers according to how in his view the hues best harmonize, and so that the work will produce greater diversity of colors and more beauty. He observes it, as I said, from one direction and then from another; one time in sunlight, other times in shade, at night, during the day or when it is almost night, under much or little light, crossways or from the opposite side.

To sum up, out of feathers they have made and still make, every day, statues, altar-pieces, and many other things of ours; they also interpose bits of gold at suitable places, making the work more beautiful and charming so that the whole world may wonder at it. They have made trimming for chasubles and mantles, covers or silk cases for crosses, for processions and for divine service, and mitres for bishops. And certainly, with no exaggeration, if these had been of gold or silver brocade, three thicknesses on rich crimson, or embroidered richly with gold or silver thread, with rubies, emeralds, and other precious stones, they would not have been more beautiful or more pleasing to look on. The craftsmen who surpass everyone in New Spain in this art are those of the province of Mechuacán.

Although the featherwork craftsmen are unquestionably excellent and demonstrate their great talent, the silversmiths of New Spain are not unworthy of our admiration for their delicate, outstanding work. They have made, and still make, unusual pieces, of a fineness very different from that of silverwork in any part of our Europe. What makes the pieces more admirable is that the silversmiths form and shape them only by means of fire, and with stone or flint, without any iron tool or anything that can help them produce that nicety and beauty. They made birds, animals, men, idols, vessels of various shapes, arms for war, beads or rosaries, necklaces, bracelets, earrings, and many other jewels worn by men and women. They make all this by pouring the molten metal into a cast. After casting it, they take out a vessel like a pitcher, or one like a kettle with its handle cast like a bell, not fastened but free to move from side to side. They take out a bird, such as a parrot, whose head, tongue, and wings move as if alive; the beak of an eagle does likewise. They take out a frog, and a fish with many scales, the gold scales alternating with silver ones, all having been cast, which astonishes our craftsmen.

They cast a gold she-monkey which plays with its hands and feet, and holds a spindle and seems to spin, or with an apple that it appears to eat—and other equally laughable objects. They may pour a plate divided into quarters, or more; one quarter is of gold, another of silver, and the secret of this is also hidden from our craftsmen. They made other excellent things, thousands more, while they were pagan, but now they make many more of our things, such as crosses, chalices, monstrances, wine vessels for Mass, vessels for the altar, and many other delicate things.

In the beginning, there would be an Indian, all wrapped up in a blanket, in their fashion, with only his eyes showing; he would be at some distance from the shop of one of our silver-smiths, dissembling and pretending to observe nothing. The silversmith would be shaping some gold or silver article, very delicate and of great craftsmanship. And the Indian, simply from seeing him make some part of the article, would go off to his house, make it himself as well or better, and soon carry it from there in his hand to sell to whoever would buy it.

They have made and copied thousands of our objects in these arts, faultlessly; therefore, all our craftsmen avoid making things in front of them. . . . As soon as the Indians saw flutes, oboes, sackbuts, and other musical instruments, they made them perfectly, without anyone teaching them. They make a sackbut out of a candlestick. I don't know whether they have made organs, but I don't doubt that they could make them, and make them well, without difficulty.

In the square of Mexico City, I myself saw an Indian with fetters on his feet, a slave, who had three or four large, excellent guitars. The ornaments, especially, were very neat and delicate, so artfully made that I stopped to look at them and also at the fetters he wore as a slave. Near him was a Spaniard, his master; I asked the Spaniard if they had brought those guitars from Castile, and I started to praise the ornaments. He replied that the maker of the guitars was the one who held them in his hand.

"And the ornaments?" I asked.

"Yes, also of the ornaments," he answered.

I remained admiring, and could not have believed him if he had not strongly affirmed his statement.

❦ 18 ❦

The Marketplace of Mexico City

The following selection, from Chapter 70 of the Apologetic History, *depicts the colorful markets of Mexico City and provides evidence of the activity of another one of the six classes required in a well-ordered republic — the men of wealth, or traders.* (Obras Escogidas, *III, 234-236.*)

A sight which can scarcely be exaggerated is that of the markets of Mexico City. This city has two districts, and in each one there is a most impressive market, in a very large square. One is called the market square or marketplace of Mexico, and the other that of Tlatelulco; the Franciscans have been located here, so we all call it Santiago. In each square there is room for over 200,000 souls; every day, especially the five [week] days, there are more than 100,000 souls in each square.

All the crafts and products there can be, throughout New Spain, are found there. There is no lack of goods to supply the natural needs, nor of things for unusual tastes. Each craft and kind of merchandise has its separate place, which no one else dares disturb or occupy. But the people who come to the markets are so numerous that the squares, even though they are large, lack space for all the merchandise; therefore, goods which cause an obstruction and take up much room, such as stone, brick, adobe or sun-baked brick, lime, sand, lumber, firewood, charcoal, and other cumbersome things are placed at the entrances of the nearest streets.

All the foodstuffs, raw and cooked, are found there. One essential product is salt, made from the water of the salt lake there and from there distributed through much of New Spain There are fabrics for cotton blankets and white woolen blankets, coarse pieces of cloth lightly or deeply colored, with rich colors, for shirts, for tablecloths, for handkerchiefs ... and for many other things. There is an abundance of clothing and footwear of many kinds.

Various fine colors are sold to those who practice the craft of painting. There are admirable featherwork goods; there are feathers of all colors, not artificially dyed, but natural. There are all the birds which go through the air or breed on land, dead or live, for whoever wishes to buy them; also animals, dead or live.

Hares, rabbits, and little dogs which do not bark but grunt and, as they say, are good to eat, are sold there. They sell deer, quartered or whole, and other animals which they hunt. There are meat and fish, boiled and roasted, the fish consisting of what they catch in the lake; also baked bread, loaves kneaded with kidney beans which are like the lupines of Castile, although not exactly the same color, for these are black and tawny and other shades. There are many other vegetables, an infinite amount of maize. A great variety of fruits are sold, and there is no counting the edible roots and greens brought here for good or for medicinal purposes.

There are many taverns one may enter in order to eat and drink their wines made from maize. ... They sell honey and must, the honey from bees and the must from agaves which ... are called *metl*. They sell wax, usually yellow and, much of it, nearly black, and this is from bees which live underground.

There are many jewels set in gold and silver, also pearls and stones like turquoise, and others. However, there are few precious stones, either because there are none naturally in that land or because the Indians do not show them. Montezuma and his lords did possess them, but they were consumed after we hastily entered. There are silk weavers who make and sell many delicate laces and other things of silk.

They sell the hides of animals, wonderfully dressed, as we say, and they also prepare the skins of birds, keeping all the feathers. They sell many kinds of snails, large and small, as well as shells, bones, and other things of this sort which they prize; also different kinds of very pretty crockery, made of painted clay; and vessels which ... they make from gourds called *hibueros* in this island of Hispaniola, so beautifully that the king will drink from them. Numberless are the products, which I do not now recall, sold in those markets of Mexico City.

Because of all the goods brought from outside ... and on account of the people coming from many places to buy them, it is thought that 50,000 or 100,000 canoes go on the lake. Canoes are small boats made from dugout logs, the prow narrower than the poop; each holds twenty, thirty, fifty and more persons. In this island of Hispaniola and in Cuba, there were very large canoes which held eighty persons. ... The word *canoe* comes from this island of Hispaniola; its name in the Mexican language was *atcale*, from *at*, meaning "water," and *cale*, meaning "house" — as if to say, "house upon water." ...

And these products are bought in exchange for others, for the most part by a barter system, according to their valuation of the merchandise. Inequalities between goods exchanged are made up by money consisting of the beans ... called cacao. It usually suffices to pay for less valuable goods with cacao.

And with this, we conclude the fourth part of our description of the self-sufficient republic, provisioned and well governed.

⁘{ 19 }⁘

A Volcano in Nicaragua

The following selection, from Chapter 112 of the Apologetic
History, *gives a detailed description of Masaya, one of the
chief volcanos of Nicaragua, which Las Casas climbed in
1536.* (Obras Escogidas, *III, 388-392.*)

Marvelous things have been said about what nature performed,
and performs, secretly, every day in the . . volcanoes of Etna
and Vesuvius; there is no one who would not feel wonder and
awe at the sight of them, and at the fire which bursts from them.
But I wish now, in this chapter, to describe another volcano,
which surpasses all that have already been mentioned, all written about by any author, past or present, and, I believe, all that
may be reported. Speaking without exaggeration, it is wonderful
beyond any there may be throughout the world.

This is the volcano they call the Inferno, in the province of
Nicaragua; or, the Inferno of Masaya, because it is near an
Indian town called Masaya by the Indians. However, another
town or towns are nearer the volcano than Masaya; perhaps that
entire region rather than the town was named Masaya. That
province we call Nicaragua, which is on the Pacific Ocean
between the port of Panama . . . and Guatemala, is among the
most fortunate in the Indies, and in the world, overflowing with
all the necessities and luxuries of human life. It has many fresh-
water lakes, large and small; there are two large ones, one forty

leagues in circumference that drains into another a hundred and more leagues around.

In a certain part of this province, three leagues from the lakes, there is a lofty mountain—it is one league to the top. Nearly all the country is fertile by nature, and at the foot of the mountain there is a little valley which cuts it off and makes it somewhat round. In one part there is a fresh-water lake a league or more in circumference, if I have not forgotten, and so deep that, as we understood there, no length of rope can reach the bottom. . . . Around the two large lakes where there are the most settlements and at the edges of the mountain and volcano, which is level, pleasant country, it is also cavernous; when one walks across the ground it reverberates as if it were all hollow. The ascent of the mountain is unobstructed and not very difficult because it can be made on horseback.

When we climbed the mountain we found it all open at the top, an opening as wide as the mountain, more than 1,500 paces in circumference, if I have not forgotten. The opening, the walls, and everything that will be described, above and below, are as visible and clear as the grand plaza of a Spanish city, because sunlight bathes everything unimpeded, just as it bathes any field and makes it bright.

This opening, the entire hole, let us say, goes down to a well, in such a way that the bottom or plaza below, soon to be described, is like the opening above, or just a little narrower. The distance from above—from what we called the opening— to the bottom and plaza below is 200 and more *estados*, [an *estado* equals 1.85 yards] as it seemed to us. The plaza below is very level, as if hand-made, and, as I said, as bright and cheerful as an open field, except that it lacks green grass.

Nearly in the middle of the plaza, but a little to one side, is a round well, appearing as if fashioned by hand. From above, the well seems to be twenty-five or thirty paces in circumference and more than thirty *estados* deep. Right there is the fire, or whatever it is, like liquefied metal from which they make cannon and bells. It is always stirring and boiling; those of us who are above at the opening hear this indistinctly. From time to time, at given moments . . . the fire billows and emits part of that metal, or whatever it is, as sparks. They strike the walls at a height of two or three *estados*, then are extinguished.

In this well many birds, many small birds are flying, apparently not far from the fire. From above we saw everything that has been described, as clearly as if we and these things were on a plain. To tell the truth, since the depth is so great and since the walls drop down from the opening as if cut by a plummet, we did not approach the edge to see more without great fear, and danger, of falling.

What I feel is most wonderful of all, unquestionably, is that, since that fire or metal is live coal, not flame, and is so deep, the vapor and brightness alone that emerges from it ascends straight up to the clouds, is seen fifty leagues away at sea, and appears to be flame that burns. To best enjoy the sight and appreciate its brightness, it is advisable to climb to the top of the mountain and sleep there overnight. This I did, because in daytime, with the sun, one does not see how bright it is.

Certain of us friars were there all one night, and I believe that we said matins without other light than what the brightness of the volcano imparted. We judged that the light it made was as strong as what the day gives on cloudy mornings. When my companion and I were in a town the Indians call Nindirí, the last syllable accented, a league and a half from the volcano, and we went walking, we thought that with our bodies we made as much of a shadow on the side opposite the glow of the volcano as we would have made if we had had an eight-day moon there.

In view of what has been said above about the natural causes of the engendering of fire in volcanoes, I believe that this fire of Masaya is caused by the violent motion of the waters of the two large lakes. For from mid-day on, and sometimes earlier, there are usually strong winds on the lakes, so strong that they raise waves as high as if this were the sea. As the lakes are only two or three leagues from the volcano, this sweep of waves must enter through certain caverns and produce wind. The wind must ignite the sulphur, and there must also be much bitumen there. Thus that fire is sustained, and, in addition, has as fuel a certain kind of metal shortly to be described.

When that fire explodes, which must be when there are great rains . . . it rises to the top with a furious roar. . . . It carries with it a vast amount of porous pumice stone and hurls the lightest stones out, and with them and the ashes scorches the land for four leagues around. In the little valley ... there are over a million cartfuls of this light, burnt pumice stone, which resembles slag from the forges of ironsmiths. . . . . And since the heavier the stone ... the shorter the distance it is cast, it follows that the top of the mountain is full of the heaviest stones, all very rough — as I said, like slag from the forges of ironsmiths. There is so much of it, all slate-colored and jagged, that on the whole mountain we scarcely found unoccupied land with room for our bodies, so we could stretch out to sleep.

These stones spread over the mountain are not separate, one from another, like the pumice stones of which I say that little valley is full and which are thrown elsewhere. But they are joined together, made into craggy rock as if formed there originally, like slate-colored boulders in rugged mountains — like points of diamonds or awls ... Near the mouth there are great fragments of stone or metal . . . , not slate-colored but almost smooth and the color of iron, or more the shade of copper than of iron. . . . I have no doubt that this metal is a kind of iron or copper, by which, as if by a substance like wood, that fire must be nourished.

The whole crowd of Spaniards who have seen that volcano have imagined that that metal, or whatever it is, which feeds that fire may be silver, gold, or some other valuable thing. For as St. Ambrose says, the greedy man fancies that everything he sees and hears of is money. For this reason, some made the king an offer to investigate what was there at their own expense, asking a reward for any good news of those things. Others worked secretly to fashion a certain apparatus with which to enter the volcano and were a year making it; having finished, four agreed to enter together. And out of curiosity, a friar was one of them.

And when the time came to go into the volcano in the wooded vessel, which they had fashioned for that purpose, and they saw that the hole was so deep and that the business was so dangerous, they were afraid. But the friar, with more rashness than courage, wished to enter alone. Having taken a cross in one hand and a hammer in the other, to break any stone along the wall below that might obstruct him, he finally arrived safe and sound beneath, and walked at his pleasure through the plaza, laughing and mocking at those who had not dared be his companions.

He carried his long ropes, a good chain at the end of them, and on that an iron helmet to collect that metal or treasure, what there was room for. When he lowered his rope, chain, and helmet, all of the chain that entered the fire, along with its helmet, shattered in an instant, like a radish cut or broken to pieces by a machete.

Very deliberately, the friar viewed all he saw of this burning metal, the fire, the depth of the well, and whatever else there was in the well. And since I knew him well, he wrote me at length while I was in Mexico City, giving me special news of all he had seen and done. Among other things he declared to me were these. First, that while from above the depth of the well down to the fire seemed to us to be 30 *estados*, it was 100 or more. Second, that the metal, or whatever it is, which seems to be burning there is not still, but that there is a river of it which flows along as if it were water. Third, that that river of metal or fire, or whatever it may be, is as wide as one of the streets of Mexico City. Any of these streets is as wide as the street in Valladolid called the *Corredera*. He wrote me other things about this which I do not remember, and I believe certainly that he wrote me nothing contrary to the truth.

⊰ 20 ⊱

The Meanings of "Barbarous"

Las Casas wrote two conclusions for the Apologetic History.
*The first, Chapter 263, asserts that "all these peoples of these
Indies" have now been shown to "equal many races of the world
that are renowned and considered civilized" and to "surpass
many others," being "inferior to none." But then, as an after-
thought, Las Casas wrote a second conclusion: five more chapters analyzing the meaning of the word "barbarous."*

*This second conclusion was an attempt to lay the ghost of
Aristotle, whom Las Casas had invoked near the beginning
of his work. For Aristotle was a two-edged sword. The Indians
could be shown to measure up to his standards in many
respects, yet Aristotle's underlying intention in his* Politics, *to
justify Greek rule over non-Greek or "barbarous" peoples,
could tell against Las Casas. Indian customs such as human
sacrifice and cannibalism might seem to invite a well-inten-
tioned Spanish conquest, an undertaking of the "white man's
burden" of forcibly uplifting an "inferior" race.*

*Therefore, without rejecting Aristotle's category of "slaves
by nature," Las Casas now attempted to prove, once for all,
that the Indians did not fall under it. The following selection,
from Chapters 264-267 and the Epilogue of the* Apologetic
History, *gives his arguments.* (Obras Escogidas, *IV, 434-437,
439-441, 445.*)

We have sometimes used this word "barbarous" above ... and
many call and consider these Indian peoples, as well as other

races, barbarous. Sometimes the word is found in Holy Scripture; barbarians are frequently named and discussed in the sacred decrees and secular histories, and the Philosopher [Aristotle] in particular makes special mention of barbarians in his *Politics*. And I often consider that an error is made in such discussions, certain barbarians being mistaken for others.

Therefore, to avoid this impropriety and confusion, I wish to explain here what it is to be barbarous and what races may properly be so called. To explain this, it is fitting to distinguish four branches, that is, four different ways in which a race or people, in whole or in part, may be called barbarous.

The first way, taking the term broadly and improperly, is because of some strangeness, ferocity, disorder, or unreasonableness ... also, because of some confused or hasty opinion, furious, tumultuous, or irrational, as when certain men, forgetting the rules of reason ... somehow become or are fierce, hardhearted and cruel; they rush to commit acts so savage that wild beasts from the forests would not do worse. These are men who seem to have stripped themselves completely of their human nature.

The second kind of barbarous people is something narrower; under it come those who do not have a written speech that corresponds to their language as Latin does to ours—in brief, who lack the use and study of letters. These peoples are said to be barbarous *secundum quid*, that is, according to some part of quality which they lack—which they would need in order not to be barbarous. For otherwise they may be wise and cultivated, not fierce nor strange nor rude. Thus, because the English lacked the use of letters and so that his countrymen would not be considered barbarous, the Venerable Bede, who was English, introduced the liberal arts in the English language, as his *History* narrates and as St. Thomas [Aquinas] also reports in his *Politics*, Book I, the first lesson.

Likewise, a man is apt to be called barbarous, in comparison with another, because he is strange in his manner of speech and mispronounces the language of the other, and also because they do not suit one another in conversation. According to Strabo, Book XIV, this was the chief reason the Greeks called other peoples barbarous, that is, because they were mispronouncing the Greek language. But from this point of view, there is no man or race which is not barbarous with respect to some other man or race. ... Thus, just as we esteemed these peoples of these Indies barbarous, so they considered us, because of not understanding us.

Las Casas here defines a subdivision of the second class of barbarians as including, "races who more than others endured the services and burdens which their kings imposed on them because of their humility."

There is a third kind of barbarous people, taking the word narrowly—very narrowly and properly: those who ... appear cruel and ferocious, remote from other men and not ruling themselves by reason. ... They neither have nor care for law, right, nation, friendship, or the company of other men, because of which they lack towns, councils, and cities, since they do not live socially. And so they neither have nor endure lords, or laws, or political rule. ... Strictly speaking, such men are called, and are, barbarous. ... These are the men of whom Aristotle particularly speaks in Book I of his *Politics*, Chapters 2 and 5, saying they are slaves by nature and should always serve and be subject to others.

There is a fourth kind of barbarous people, which can be deduced from what has been said above: it includes all those who lack true religion and the Christian faith, that is, all pagans, however wise and prudent they may be as philosophers and statesmen.

However, there is a distinct difference among pagans, as the Doctors declare and we also see by experience, because [1] there are certain pagans and barbarians who suffer from a purely negative infidelity, that is, who never heard the news of Christ and of our faith or teaching. ... Their infidelity does not bear the stigma of sin insofar as it consists of not possessing the faith of Jesus Christ.

But [2] there are other pagans and barbarians whose infidelity if different from this. ... Their infidelity is called—and is—

contrary or opposite, in accordance with their opposition to the faith. That is, having heard the news of the Gospel, they refuse to receive it and knowingly resist its preaching, through pure hatred of our faith and of the name of Christ. They not only refuse to hear and receive it, but they attack and persecute it, and, to enhance and spread their own sect, would destroy it if they could. In them the principle and sin of real infidelity is perfected.

From all this it will be easy to comprehend under which kind all these Indian races of ours are included. ... We may say that these peoples of these Indies are not under the first kind, because that kind results from chance, not nature. ... Such defects could not naturally befall an entire race ... so that all men of a race would be raging, weak-minded, or blind with passion. ... Clearly, neither are these Indian peoples under the third kind, because they have their kingdoms and their kings, their way of life, their well-governed and well-ordered republics, their houses and estates, and they live under laws.

Nor are they under the second subdivision of the fourth kind, because they never injured the Church, nor understood or had news that there was a Church in the world, nor knew what the Christian people were until we went to seek them; they had their lands, provinces, kingdoms, and kings far apart from ours, as everyone knows, each town and province living at peace.

It follows, therefore, that broadly speaking all these peoples are barbarous only according to a certain quality, and first, insofar as they are pagans, merely through lacking our holy faith — a so-called purely negative infidelity which is not a sin, as has been stated. Thus they are included under the fourth kind. They are also included under the second kind, owing to three conditions: first, inasmuch as they lacked letters (or communication by letters, like the English); second, because they are very humble peoples, who obey their kings in a strange and admirable manner; third, through not speaking our language well, nor understanding us — but in this, we are as barbarous to them as they are to us.

These, then, are the numberless peoples or races of the western and southern Indies . . . which that eminent man Don Christopher Columbus discovered, first opening the enclosure that for so many thousands of years the Ocean Sea had possessed, for which he worthily became its first Admiral.

PART IV

POLITICAL THINKER

MEMORIALS AND TREATISES

In addition to the *History of the Indies* and the *Apologetic History*, Las Casas wrote many treatises, letters, and memorials addressed to the king or his ministers, etc., in which he expressed his ideas about Indian problems and Spain's rights and duties in the New World. Among these writings is the one which gained him the most fame, or notoriety, during his own life, the *Very Brief Account of the Destruction of the Indies*. Today, however, scholars consider another work, of which only a fragment is extant, The *Only Method of Attracting All People to the True Faith*, to be a more important exposition of Las Casas' system of ideas—almost as important as the two histories.

Las Casas' system of political thought is firmly based on the "fundamental concepts of medieval Europe," Lewis Hanke points out. "Las Casas believed that all men originally were free, since individual liberty is a right conceded by God as an essential attribute of man. As for papal authority, he held that the pope has only voluntary jurisdiction over non-Christians, and cannot force them to accept Christianity, for this would be to follow Mahomet's method. . . . Furthermore, the pope has no authority to deprive non-Christians of their lands or property, but his right and duty is limited to dividing among Christian kings the authority over the infidel world necessary to . . . preach the faith. . . . The Spanish kings to whom America was entrusted had the same attributes and responsibilities as medieval kings, who were but the rectors or administrators of public affairs."[1]

The following selections from Las Casas' miscellaneous writings illustrate the application of these principles.

NOTE

1. Lewis Hanke, *Bartolomé de Las Casas* (The Hague: Martinus Nijhoff, 1951), pp. 36, 40.

⁓{ 21 }⁓

A New World Utopia

Sir Thomas More's Utopia, *a description of an imaginary society located somewhere in the New World, appeared in 1516. In the same year, in his* Memorial Concerning Remedies for the Indies, *Las Casas drew up a plan for an Indian utopia — a "community scheme" for integrating the flesh and blood inhabitants of the New World into Spanish Christian society. It would replace the virtual slavery of the encomienda system.*

Las Casas would take the Indians away from the encomenderos and settle them in villages of 1,000 each. A group of such villages, placed around a central Spanish town, would form a community. Directed by salaried Spanish supervisors, the Indians would labor in the mines and fields, and with the Spaniards would form a kind of joint stock company to share profits. A "chief administrator" would be in charge of all communities in any one island.

Unlike More's communistic Utopia, Las Casas' plan provided for private property, which the natives would acquire. They would intermarry with the Spaniards and ultimately become "free vassals." The following selection, from the Memorial Concerning Remedies for the Indies *(1516), gives further details. (*Obras Escogidas, *V, 16, 19-24.)*

[Hospitals]

Let there be built in each Spanish town or city a hospital called
. . . the Hospital of the King. Let it be made in the form of a

cross, with four wings, so that fifty cots or beds can be contained in each wing, so that there are 200 beds for sick Indians. And in the center of the four wings let there be an altar, so that all can follow Mass from their beds. And let the hospitals be made of very good wood, nailed with iron nails, and roofed with thatch or reed.

And in order that sick Indians may be assisted, relieved, and cured of their illnesses, and so that they do not perish because of lack of care and medicine, as they have until now, . . . let the said hospital be supplied in this way. . . . Let there always be in it a physician, a surgeon, and a pharmacist, with a shop well provided with everything usually available to cure illnesses; and let the said physicians be charged with healing the sick Indians with great diligence and kindness.

Let there be many birds, hens, and chickens at the said hospital for food. . . . Let the hospital have the 200 beds already mentioned and a mattress for each one. . . . Let them have two sheets, . . . and let each bed have a blanket. . . .

Likewise, let the hospital be provided with wooden dishes and bowls, which those who make the troughs to collect gold can make, and with dishes and bowls of clay, as needed. Indian women there are certain to make them very well out of clay — also pots and pans and everything needed that is made out of clay. And for this, let there be Indian women in the hospital, noted potters, who are paid a fair wage. And as time passes if the officials see that it is necessary to send to Spain for iron frying pans and copper pots, they will do so.

And let there be in the said hospital, along with the two Spanish hospital managers, four or six Indians, or as many as needed, so that the sick can be well waited on. Let the women needed as cooks be the wives of those same Indians who are on duty there, and let them be paid for their services. . . .

If any Indian falls sick or feels ill-disposed, let the farmers, miners, and all other persons who are employed in the . . . communities be obliged, subject to certain punishment, to send him to the hospital, or to make it known immediately to some superintendent or to the hospital managers. . . . And if there are muleteers present, let them at once carry such sick or ill-disposed Indians from wherever they find them to the said hospital. . . .

And let there always be two or three beasts of burden at the hospital, or as many as are needed, to be sent out to bring in any sick Indian.

[Labor Regulations]

To support all that concerns them and to serve ... the Crown, it is necessary that the Indians work—but moderately, so that for that purpose they do not decline or die, as they have until the present. Therefore, let the method followed in such work ... be this. First, let the Indians who will toil on farmlands and estates, and at other tasks that do not involve collecting gold, work six months of the year, working two months and then resting two. And each day when they have to eat, allow them to rest four hours; bring them to eat at ten o'clock and return them to work after two o'clock.

And do this the year round, for it is very sunny there and, on account of the great heat which causes the Indians much suffering, is really summer all year round. And if, in the days of May, June, July, and August, they are given five hours of relief, it is sure to be very beneficial to them. ... And in order that this can better be carried out, let them have sand-glasses [hourglasses]. ...

Let the Indians be distributed in such a way that a certain number, as many as needed, stay in their villages to do their own farming. ... Let some Indians remain, so many to each *bohio* or house, according to the judgment of the attorney, to bring food to women, children, and old persons, and provide for them by hunting and fishing and in other necessary ways, so that they do not die of hunger, as they have until now. ...

From year to year, let the Indians shift thus: let those who will remain this year to do their own farming, to serve, and to provide food for the women, children, and old ones, go next year to serve the community as described on Spanish farmlands and estates; and let those who have already served in the said community stay at home, because thus all the Indians will work and rest equally.

Since it will be necessary to make cotton shirts and hammocks ... let Indian men be taught to make such dry goods ... or let the women be paid for their labor. ... Let each one be given so much per pound or per arroba of cotton that she spins and, likewise, so much for each shirt or hammock that she makes. Let the women do it at their leisure and not be hurried, as they have been until the present, so that an infinite number have died, having been made to spin or weave all day without getting up from one place and without being given anything to eat. And let them have liberty and know that they do not have to serve or work if they do not wish to. ...

As for the Indians who will have to work in the mines ... of the 2,000 more or less, which each community can send out to collect gold, let half be assigned to do so for two months; and when the two months are ended, let them come back to rest the next two. Then let the other half, who were resting, go to work and serve for the specified time. Thus, continuously, half of them will be in the mines collecting gold and half resting, and this for eight months. When eight months have passed, let the smelting of the gold take place, and let all the Indians of the mines rest for two months while the smelting lasts. When that is finished, let half the Indians return to the mines, the other half remaining to rest.

Let them be permitted to rest and divert themselves certain hours each day, at meal time, as described for the Indians who must work at farming. And let all Indians who go in the mines always be well clothed, because they go ever in water and cold.

Let no Indian be taken to collect gold who is under twenty-five years of age or over forty-five, because the work ... is very hard and not suitable for any except strong, robust fellows. And let no community have the power to turn out to the said mines or compel to collect gold more than a third of the Indian males of this age, for they could send out too many, so that there would be no one to do the farming and thus they would suffer hunger.

Let no Indians be taken to cultivate the soil or to collect gold more than fifteen or twenty leagues from their settlements and towns. ... For in this short a distance, the land will not try them, and in going and coming they will not be left dead along the roads, as they have been until now. . . . Also, let a superintendent always go with all the Indians who have to walk from mines or farmlands to their homes to rest; and let food supplies be carried for them in the mule trains of the communities, so that they do not lack food or suffer hunger en route to their country and villages.

Do not allow the Indians to work with wooden hoes, in the mines or on the estates or anywhere else. . . . The Spaniards now make them work with these, and make them level mounds with their stone hatchets; as a result they toil much more than if they worked with hoes, spades, and hatchets of iron. . . . Let no pack be loaded on any Indian either because the road is a bad one or a good one, or is one where beasts of burden can or cannot go; instead, let all loads, large and small, be absolutely prohibited. . . . Likewise, do not permit the Indians to pump out ships, as they have done in Cuba, because thus they crush their bodies and waste away around the liver.

Let no Indian go out to serve anywhere who does not carry his hammock with him to sleep in. Let a couch be made, with plenty of straw, for him who at present does not have a hammock. . . . Let the hammocks and couches be placed quite high above the ground, because of the dampness. And let no Indian be permitted to sleep on the ground, but let him who does be punished for it, if necessary; let special care be taken for those in the mines.

❧{ 22 }❧

The "Only Method" of Converting the Indians

On June 9, 1537, Pope Paul III issued his bull Sublimis Deus, *which declared "that the Indians are truly men and that they are . . . capable of understanding the Catholic faith." It further stated that "the said Indians . . . are by no means to be deprived of their liberty or . . . their property . . . nor should they be in any way enslaved.* *

Las Casas' The Only Method of Attracting All People to the True Faith, *written in Latin in the 1530s, draws the logical conclusion that the conversion of such free men should be by peaceful means. Following the example and precepts of Christ, preachers should convert nonbelievers "by persuading the understanding . . . and by attracting the will,"*** *as Las Casas did in his mission to Tuzulutlán. Las Casas refutes the theory of conquistadors and worldly ecclesiastics like Bishop Fonseca that the Indians should first be subjected, then converted.*

From Bartolomé de Las Casas, *Del Único Modo de Atraer a Todos los Pueblos a la Verdadera Religión,* ed. Augustín Millares Carlo (Mexico City: Fondo de Cultura Económica, 1942). Reprinted by permission.

**Sublimis Deus,* quoted in Lewis Hanke, *The Spanish Struggle for Justice in the Conquest of America* (Boston: Little, Brown, 1965), p. 73.
**Bartolomé de Las Casas, *Del Único Modo de Atraer a Todos los Pueblos a la Verdadera Religión,* p. 6.

Only Chapters 5, 6, and 7 of Book I of this treatise, Las
Casas' first major work, are extant. The following selection,
from this fragment of the treatise, gives some of the basic
principles of modern missionary activity. (Del Único Modo
de Atraer a Todos los Pueblos a la Verdadera Religión,
pp. 6-9, 248-255, 260-261, 396-401.)

[The Only Method of Teaching the True Religion]

The one and only method of teaching men the true religion was
established by Divine Providence for the whole world, and for
all times, that is, by persuading the understanding through reasons, and by gently attracting or exhorting the will. This method
should be common to all men throughout the world, without any
distinction made for sects, errors, or corrupt customs.

This conclusion will be proved in many ways by arguments
drawn from reason; by examples of the ancient Fathers; by the
rule and manner of preaching which Christ instituted for all
times; by the practices of the Apostles; by quotations from holy
teachers; by the most ancient tradition of the Church and by her
numerous ecclesiastical decrees.

And first, this conclusion will be proved by arguments drawn
from reason, among which let this be the first. There is only one
method peculiar to Divine Wisdom by which it disposes and
moves created beings gently to actions and to their natural ends.
But among created beings, rational creatures are higher and
more excellent than all others which were not made in the image
of God. . . . Therefore, Divine Wisdom moves rational creatures,
that is, men, to their actions or operations gently. . . . Therefore,
the method of teaching men the true religion ought to be gentle,
enticing, and pleasant. This method is by persuading the understanding and by attracting the will.

[How To Preach the Gospel]

One can deduce five integral or essential parts which make up
or constitute the form of preaching the Gospel in accordance
with the intention and precepts of Christ.

The first, according to Chrysostom, is that hearers, especially pagans, should understand that the preachers of the faith have no intention of acquiring power over them through their preaching. Chrysostom said that, therefore, he never used the language of flattery, nor any deceit, in his preaching—devices of seducers attempting to invade and rule. For it cannot be said that we flatter in order to rule, which is what these words refer to: "Nor have we sought glory from men, neither from you nor from others" [1 Thess. 2, 6]. . . . Thus [St. Paul] says all this to remove any suspicion, as Chrysostom affirms.

The second part is that hearers, especially pagans, should understand that no desire for riches moves them to preach. And therefore it is said, "Nor any pretext for avarice" [1 Thess. 2, 5], that is, according to Anselm, we have not preached with the purpose of seeking an occasion of seizing your goods for ourselves; we have kept in mind the words of the Lord by which he forbade the Apostles to possess gold, silver, or money, thus plucking out the root of all evils. For as Jerome says in his commentary on Matthew, if they had taken those goods, it could appear that they were preaching not for the salvation of men but to enrich themselves; and consequently, their teaching would have been disparaged, being considered a doubtful truth. . . .

The third part is that in speaking and conversing with their hearers, especially pagans, the preachers should show themselves so mild and humble, courteous and . . . good-willed that the hearers eagerly wish to listen and hold their teaching in greater reverence. For this reason, it is said "We have been made children," or, according to Chrysostom, as I said, "gentle." "We have not left a sign of anything burdensome, troublesome, weighty, or that would seem to show superiority," according to Chrysostom in his Second Homily on the forementioned Epistle.

From what has been said, the fourth part of the form of preaching, which is more essential than the preceding, may clearly be deduced. This is that the preaching be fruitful to the preachers, that is, that they possess that same love of charity by which Paul was accustomed to love all the men in the world, so that they might be saved. The sisters of that charity are mildness, patience, and kindness. "Charity is patient, is kind, bears with all things, endures all things," etc. (1 Cor. 13, 4, 7).

The fifth part is contained in the words of Paul. . . , "You are witnesses and God also, how holy and just and blameless was our conduct towards you who have believed" [1 Thess. 2, 10] — before as well as after your conversion, as the interlineal gloss says.

According to the interlineal gloss and St. Athanasius, the words "how holy" mean how holy with respect to God, that is, we have done all that it was necessary to do, observing the respect owed God in piety and worship. . . . The words "how just" refer to our neighbor, toward whom we must act in the way that is owed, and not the opposite; according to the interlineal gloss and Athanasius, they mean by doing injury to no one, not demanding money. "Blameless" means without offending anyone.

[Conquest: The Wrong Method of Conversion]

A method contrary to the one we have been defending would be the following: that . . . the pagans should first be subjected, whether they wished to be or not, to the rule of the Christian people, and that once they were subjected, organized preaching would follow. In this case, the preachers would not compel them to believe but would convince them by arguments and also draw them gently, once the many impediments which preaching could encounter had been removed by the said subjection.

But since no pagan, above all no pagan kings, would wish voluntarily to submit to the rule of a Christian people, or of any prince, it would certainly be necessary to come to a war.

However, war brings with it these evils: the crash of arms; sudden attacks and invasions, impetuous and furious; violence and deadly confusion; licentiousness, deaths and massacres; rapine, pillage and plunder; parents deprived of their sons, and sons of their parents; captivities; kings and natural lords deprived of their estates and dominions; the devastation and desolation of

innumerable towns and cities. And all these evils fill kingdoms
. . . with sad laments.

Laws are silent, humane feelings are mocked, nowhere is
there rectitude, religion is an object of scorn, and there is absolutely no distinction made between the sacred and the profane.
War also fills every place with highwaymen, thieves, ravishers,
fires, and murders. Indeed, what is war but general murder and
robbery among many? And the more widespread it is, the more
criminal it is. Through war extreme misfortune is brought upon
thousands of innocents who do not deserve the injury that is
done them. To sum up, in war men lose their riches, their bodies,
and their souls.

But now we have to see how this method of preaching the
faith is contrary to the one indicated above, and also that it is
the most unsuitable method of all . . . for attracting and enticing
peoples to the congregation of Christ. . . . This is proved first by
the following argument . . . .

A rational creature has a natural capacity for being moved,
directed and drawn to any good gently . . . because of his freedom of choice. But if pagans find themselves first injured,
oppressed, saddened, and afflicted by the misfortunes of wars,
through the loss of their children, their goods, and their own
liberty . . . how can they be moved voluntarily to listen to what
is proposed to them about faith, religion, justice, and truth? Or
how will they be able to adhere to what has been preached?
Likewise, if a soft word multiplies friends and, on the contrary,
"An ill-tempered man stirs up strife" (Prov. 15, 18), how many
enemies will not such bitter words and works make? . . .

Therefore, if man, this same rational creature . . . ought to
be guided and persuaded to good, especially the good of faith
and religion, gently and mildly, but as a result of wars . . . is, on
the contrary, compelled in a harsh, bitter and violent manner,
it is clear that such means, unnatural and contrary to the condition of human nature, will produce contrary effects. That is,
man will not wish to hear the truths of the faith and will scorn
what is said to him. For if men are forced to listen, they will not

want to give assent to what they have heard ... since no one believes unless he wishes to. ...

For if things which are gentle, mild, and pleasing cause a man to listen to new matters willingly ... and to lend faith to what he hears, contrary things must produce a contrary effect. Therefore, this method of subjecting pagans by war to the rule of the Christian people so that the Gospel may be preached to them is contrary to the natural and gentle method described earlier.

❧{ 23 }❧

A "Very Brief Account" of Spanish Cruelty

Las Casas composed his best known work, the Very Brief Account of the Destruction of the Indies, *while lobbying at the court of Charles V for reforms for the Indians from 1540 to 1542. It is a chronicle, resembling the medieval chronicles with which Las Casas was familiar; even its title, "the Destruction of the Indies," is an adaptation of the phrase used by medieval writers for the Moslem conquest of Spain—"the destruction of Spain."**

The Very Brief Account of the Destruction of the Indies *not only helped create the atmosphere for Charles V's "Emancipation Proclamation"—the New Laws of 1542—but also spread the "Black Legend" of Spanish cruelty. Written in 1542 and published in 1552, it was translated into six other European languages by 1626. In 1598, Theodore De Bry made famous illustrations for its lurid scenes. It soon became part of the propaganda of Spain's rivals and was used for this purpose as late as 1898. In that year, an English translation*

From Francis Augustus MacNutt, Bartolomew de Las Casas (Cleveland: Arthur H. Clark, 1909).

*Lewis Hanke, "Estudio Preliminar" in Bartolomé de Las Casas, *Historia de las Indias,* ed. Augustín Millares Carlo (Mexico City: Fondo de Cultura Económica, 1951), I, lxxv.

*was printed in New York in connection with the Spanish-
American War—an edition containing De Bry's illustrations,
but with one page left blank and an explanation that the picture for that page was too horrible to reproduce! Las Casas'
statistics are exaggerated (see p. 25); his conclusions about
Spanish oppression are still hotly debated, although it has been
pointed out that he based his work on official reports to the
Crown.*

The following selection from the Very Brief Account of
the Destruction of the Indies *illustrates Las Casas' eloquence and his indignation at the sufferings of the Indians.*
(Obras Escogidas, *V. 135-137, 142-144, 163.*)

The Destruction of the Indies

The Indies were discovered in the year 1492. The year following,
Spanish Christians went to inhabit them, so that it is since forty-
nine years that numbers of Spaniards have gone there: and the
first land, that they invaded to inhabit, was the large and most
delightful isle of Hispaniola, which has a circumference of 600
leagues.

There are numberless other islands, and very large ones . . .
that were all—and we have seen it—as inhabited and full of
their native Indian peoples as any country in the world. Of the
continent . . . more than 10,000 leagues of maritime coast have
been discovered, and more is discovered every day; all that has
been discovered up to the year 1549 is full of people, like a hive
of bees. . . .

God has created all these numberless people to be quite the
simplest, without malice or duplicity, most obedient, most faithful to their natural lords, and to the Christians, whom they serve.
. . . They are likewise the most delicate people, weak and of
feeble constitution, and less than any other can they bear
fatigue. . . . They are also a very poor people, who of worldly
goods possess little, nor wish to possess; and they are therefore
neither proud, nor ambitious, nor avaricious.

Their food is so poor, that it would seem that of the Holy

Fathers in the desert was not scantier nor less pleasing. Their way of dressing is usually to go naked, covering the private parts. ... Their beds are of matting, and they mostly sleep in certain things like hanging nets, called in the language of Hispaniola *hamacas*.

They are likewise of a clean, unspoiled, and vivacious intellect, very capable, and receptive to every good doctrine; most prompt to accept our Holy Catholic Faith, to be endowed with virtuous customs.

Among these gentle sheep ... the Spaniards entered ... like wolves, tigers, and lions which had been starving for many days, and since forty years they have done nothing else; nor do they otherwise at the present day, than outrage, slay, afflict, torment, and destroy them. ... To such extremes has this gone that, whereas there were more than 3 million souls, whom we saw in Hispaniola, there are today, not 200 of the native population left.

The island of Cuba is almost as long as the distance from Valladolid to Rome; it is now almost entirely deserted. The islands of San Juan [Puerto Rico] and Jamaica ... are both desolate. The Lucaya Isles lie near Hispaniola and Cuba to the north and number more than sixty. ... The poorest of these ... contained more than 500,000 souls, but today there remains not even a single creature. All were killed in transporting them to Hispaniola, because it was seen that the native population there was disappearing.

We are assured that our Spaniards, with their cruelty and execrable works, have depopulated and made desolate the great continent, and that more than ten kingdoms, larger than all Spain . . . . although formerly full of people, are now deserted.

We give as a real and true reckoning, that in the said forty years, more than 12 million persons, men, and women, and children, have perished unjustly and through tyranny, by the infernal deeds and tyranny of the Christians. ...

Two ordinary and principal methods have the self-styled Christians, who have gone there, employed in extirpating these miserable nations. ... The one, by unjust, cruel, and tyrannous wars. The other, by slaying all those who might aspire to ...

liberty or to escape from the torments that they suffer, such as all the native lords and adult men. . . .

The reason why the Christians have killed and destroyed such infinite numbers of souls is solely because they have made gold their ultimate aim, seeking to load themselves with riches in the shortest time. . . . These lands, being so happy and so rich, and the people so humble, so patient, and so easily subjugated, they have . . . taken no more account of them . . . than — I will not say of animals, for would to God they had considered and treated them as animals — but as even less than the dung in the streets.

In this way have they cared for their lives — and for their souls: and therefore, all the millions above mentioned have died without faith and without sacraments. And it is . . . admitted . . . by all . . . that the Indians throughout the Indies never did any harm to the Christians: they even esteemed them as coming from heaven, until they and their neighbors had suffered the same many evils, thefts, deaths, violence, and visitations at their hands. . . .

The Island of Cuba

In the year 1511 the Spaniards passed over to the island of Cuba . . . where there were great and populous provinces. They began and ended in the above manner, only with incomparably greater cruelty. Here many notable things occurred.

A very high prince and lord, named Hatuey, who had fled with many of his people from Hispaniola to Cuba, to escape the calamity and inhuman operations of the Christians, having received news from some Indians that the Christians were crossing over, assembled many or all of his people and addressed them thus.

"You already know that it is said the Christians are coming here; and you have experience of how they have treated the lords so and so and those people of Hayti (which is Hispaniola); they come to do the same here. Do you know perhaps why they do it?"

The people answered no; except that they were by nature cruel and wicked.

"They do it," said he, "not alone for this, but because they have a God whom they greatly adore and love; and to make us adore Him they strive to subjugate us and take our lives." He had near him a basket full of gold and jewels and he said, "Behold here is the God of the Christians, let us perform *Areytos* before Him, if you will (these are dances in concert and singly); and perhaps we shall please Him, and He will command that they do us no harm."

All exclaimed; it is well! it is well! They danced before it, till they were all tired, after which the lord Hatuey said: "Note well that in any event if we preserve the gold, they will finally have to kill us, to take it from us: let us throw it into this river." They all agreed to this proposal, and they threw the gold into a great river in that place.

This prince and lord continued retreating before the Christians when they arrived at the island of Cuba, because he knew them, but when he encountered them he defended himself; and at last they took him. And merely because he fled from such iniquitous and cruel people and defended himself ... with all his people and offspring until death, they burnt him alive.

When he was tied to the stake, a Franciscan friar, a holy man who was there, spoke as much as he could to him, in the little time that the executioner granted them, about God and some of the teachings of our faith. ... He told him that if he would believe what was told him, he would go to heaven where there was glory and eternal rest; and if not, that he would go to hell, to suffer perpetual torments and punishment.

After thinking a little, Hatuey asked the friar whether the Christians went to heaven; the friar answered that those who were good went there. The prince at once said, without any more thought, that he did not wish to go there, but rather to hell so as not to be where Spaniards were, nor to see such cruel people.

This is the renown and honor that God and our faith have acquired by means of the Christians who have gone to the Indies. ...

The Mainland

In the year 1514 they passed over to the continent an unhappy Governor [Pedrarias Dávila] who was the cruelest of tyrants. ...

His intention was to settle large numbers of Spaniards in that country. And although several tyrants had visited the continent and had robbed and scandalized many people . . . this man surpassed all the others.

The most pernicious blindness of those who have governed the Indies up to the present day, in providing for the conversion and salvation of these people . . . reached such depths that they have commanded notice to be given the Indians to accept the holy faith and render obedience to the kings of Castile; otherwise war would be made on them with fire and blood, and they would be killed and made slaves, etc.

As though the Son of God, who died for each of them, had commanded in his law, when he said "Go and make disciples of all nations" (Matt. 28, 19), that a requirement should be sent to peaceful and quiet infidels, in their own countries, that, if they did not receive it at once . . . and . . . did not subject themselves to the dominion of a king, of whom they had never heard . . . whose messengers are so cruel . . . they should therefore lose their rights, their lands and liberty, their wives and children, with all their lives. . . .

This wretched and unhappy governor, in giving instructions as to the said requirement, the better to justify them . . . commanded these thieves sent by him, to act as follows: when they had determined to invade and plunder some province, where they had heard that gold was to be found, they should go when the Indians were in their towns and safe in their houses; these wretched Spanish assassins went by night, and halting at midnight half a league from the town, they published or read the said requirement among themselves saying: "Princes and Indians of such a place in this continent, we make known unto you that there is one God, one Pope, and one King of Castile, who is Lord of this country; come at once to render him obedience, etc.; otherwise know that we shall make war on you, kill you, and put you into slavery, etc."

And toward sunrise, the innocent natives being still asleep with their wives and children, they attacked the town, setting fire to the houses that were usually of straw, burning the children, the women, and many others alive, before they awoke.

They killed whom they would, and ... the others that survived, they put into chains as slaves. Then when the fire was extinguished or low they went to look for the gold that was in the houses. ...

The Pearl Coast

... The tyranny exercised by the Spaniards upon the Indians in fishing pearls is as cruel and reprehensible a thing as there can be in the world. Upon the land there is no life so infernal and hopeless as to be compared to it, although that of digging gold in the mines is the hardest and worst.

They let them down into the sea three and four and five fathoms deep, from morning till sunset. They are always swimming under water without respite, gathering the oysters, in which the pearls grow.

They come up to breathe bringing little nets full of them; there is a hangman Spaniard in a boat, and if they linger resting, he beats them with his fists, and taking them by the hair, throws them in the water to go on fishing.

Their food is fish and the fish that contain the pearls, and a little cassava or maize bread. ... Instead of giving them beds at night, they put them in stocks on the ground, to prevent them from escaping.

Many times the Indians throw themselves into the sea while fishing or hunting pearls and never come up again, because dolphins and sharks, which are two kinds of very cruel sea animals that swallow a man whole, kill and eat them.

From this it may be seen, whether the Spaniards, who thus seek profit from the pearls, observe the divine precepts of love to God and one's neighbor; out of avarice, they put their fellow creatures in danger of death to the body and also to the soul, because they die without faith and without sacraments.

They lead the Indians such a wretched life that they ruin and waste them in a few days; for it is impossible for men to live much under water without respiration, especially because the cold of the water penetrates their bodies, and so they generally all die of hemorrhages, oppression of the chest caused by staying such long stretches of time without breathing, and from dysentery caused by the frigidity.

Their hair, which is by nature black, changes to an ashen color like the skin of seals, and brine comes out from their shoulders so that they resemble human monsters of some species.

❧{ 24 }❧

Abolish the Encomienda!

One of Las Casas' most devastating attacks upon the encomienda is the memorial Among the Remedies, *written in 1542 as part of his campaign for the New Laws. The encomienda system of forced labor by the Indians had been introduced by Columbus in 1499, institutionalized by Nicolás de Ovando in 1503, and further implemented by the Law of Two Lives in 1536. The Law of Two Lives permitted colonists to leave their encomiendas to their wives or children for one life.*

When Las Casas read Among the Remedies *at court in 1542, it included a number of proposed reforms, such as building roads so Indians would not be used as carriers, resettling the Indians in sparsely-inhabited regions, etc. But when he printed it, he gave only the basic "Eighth Remedy" — the abolition of the encomienda. The following selection, from* Among the Remedies *(1542, published 1552), includes four of Las Casas' "twenty reasons" for doing away with the system.* (Obras Escogidas, *V, 69-70, 72-73, 76, 100-102, 117-118.*)

Among the remedies for the reformation of the Indies which Don Fray Bartolomé de las Casas, bishop of the Royal City of Chiapa, submitted at the command of the emperor king, our lord, in the councils . . . in Valladolid, in the year 1542, the eighth in order is the following: in which twenty reasons are assigned, through which he proves that the Indians ought not to

151

be given to the Spaniards in encomienda, nor in fief, nor in vassalage, nor in any other manner if His Majesty wishes, as he does, to free them, as if from the mouth of dragons, from the tyranny and destruction they suffer. . . .

The eighth remedy and, among all, the most essential because without it all the others would be worth nothing . . . is this: that Your Majesty order . . . that all the Indians in all the Indies . . . be placed, brought back, and incorporated under the royal crown of Castile and Leon, under the headship of Your Majesty, as subjects and free vassals, which they are, and that none be entrusted to Spanish Christians. . . .

And this is necessary for the following twenty reasons:

First Reason

Since certain kingdoms and their peoples, solely because they are pagans and need to be converted to our holy faith, have been committed and entrusted by God and by the Holy Apostolic See in his name to the sovereigns of Castile and Leon . . . so that the sovereigns may attract and persuade them to come to the knowledge of Jesus Christ . . . , no one is qualified to have the care of those souls who is not the king of Castile.

And that Your Majesty may see how deeply the most serene and blessed queen, Doña Isabella, your most worthy lady grandmother, felt and esteemed this obligation to be generous to your Indian vassals, may Your Majesty know that in the year 1499, the first admiral, Don Christopher Columbus . . . because of distinguished services which certain persons had performed in the island of Hispaniola . . . gave each one of them an Indian and permission to bring the Indian here to Spain with him. And I who am writing this had one of the Indians.

When the persons came back here and this was known by Her Highness, she became so angry that no one could pacify her, and she said: "What power does my Admiral have to give my vassals to anyone?" And immediately she ordered it proclaimed in Granada, where the court was at that season, that all who had brought Indians from the Indies on the first voyage should return them there, under pain of death. And in the year 1500, when the commander Francisco de Bobadilla went to govern, all restored them, and mine was returned also. . . .

Second Reason

. . . Since the purpose of the dominion of Your Majesty over those peoples is the preaching and establishing of the faith among them, and their conversion and knowledge of Christ, this and no other . . . , Your Majesty is therefore obliged to remove all obstacles that can hinder the attainment of this purpose. . . . But one of the greatest obstacles and impediments that there has been until now . . . has been for the Christians to hold them in encomiendas. The same and much worse could be said if they were given to the Christians as vassals. As proof of this we give three reasons.

The first, which has been manifest to everyone, is the great greed and avarice of the Spaniards, because of which they neither wish nor permit the religious to enter the towns of Indians entrusted to them. For they say they receive chiefly two injuries from this. One, that . . . when the religious preach to the Indians, the Spaniards lose them because of the Indians' being idle and not going to work on the estates. And it has happened that there were Indians in a church listening to a sermon and the religious preaching to them, and a Spaniard entered before all and took fifty or a hundred of them whom he needed to carry loads from his estate. And because they did not wish to go, he gave them kicks and blows with a stick in spite of them and the religious, scandalizing all the people there and hindering the salvation of both Spaniards and Indians.

The other injury which they say they receive is that after the Indians have been instructed and made Christians, they become babblers; they know more than they knew, and because of that the Spaniards cannot profit so much by them thenceforth as before. . . .

Third Reason

The Spaniards are not fit or competent agents to be entrusted with the Indians, nor to be given the office of pastor nor of preaching the faith. ... The Indians are handed over indifferently to the Christians by a cedula of encomienda which says: let there be committed or entrusted to you, so and so, so many Indians in such a town or such a town, so that you may make use of them in your mines and undertakings, extracting gold and profiting; provided that you have the duty of teaching and instructing them in matters of our holy Catholic faith; and with this I discharge His Majesty's conscience and mine

What preaching and instruction, most high Lord, and consequently what discharge of Your Majesty's conscience and that of the wretched governors can be effected by Juan Colmenero in Santa Marta, a man ... to whom they gave a large town in encomienda and made him pastor of the souls in it? He who, when he was examined by one of our friars once, did not know how to make the sign of the cross, and when asked what he was teaching the Indians of his town, answered that he gave them to the devil, that it sufficed to say to them: "by the sign of the holy cross."

What kind of preacher and pastor will that Christian be, Lord, who, after the Indians of a certain province had surrendered their idols to the religious and had declared that they wished to be servants of the true God, Christ, brought loads of idols from other regions to the market to sell and barter them for slaves to the same Indians? What kind of pastors of those souls will all the secular Spaniards who go there be ... who scarcely know the Creed and the Ten Commandments ... and who for the most part are vicious men ... in comparison with whom the Indians are very virtuous and saintly?

For the Indians, although pagans, have one wife as taught by nature and necessity, but they see those who call themselves Christians with fourteen, and many more, which the law of God forbids. And the Indians take from no one what is his; they neither exhaust, nor injure, nor kill anyone, but they see Christians commit every crime. ...

Eleventh Reason

The encomienda system, giving Indians to the Spaniards, always lacked the authority of the sovereigns. And he who first devised it, dividing the Indians in this island of Hispaniola generally among the Spaniards as if they were herds of cattle, thus depopulating and destroying this island, never had the power to do so but exceeded the limits of his orders ... This was the chief commander of Alcántara and the commander of Lares [Nicolás de Ovando], whom, in the year 1502, the two most serene Catholic sovereigns Don Ferdinand and Doña Isabella sent from the city of Granada to govern Hispaniola. ... This governor carried among his instructions strict orders from Their Highnesses that he should rule the Indians as free men, with much love, forbearance, charity and justice, not imposing any slavery on them. ...

Three thousand Spaniards arrived with the commander of Lares in the said island. As he held them in the city of Santo Domingo, where they had disembarked with him, he did not know how to contrive to distribute them throughout the land among the Indians, so that they would have something to eat. Thus they began to be hungry. Soon he thought of what seemed to him a remedy, and not being able to carry it out because of his orders to govern the Indians as free men, he wrote the most serene queen many things against the Indians, falsely ... to influence Her Highness to give him permission to parcel them out, as he had schemed.

And among other things, he wrote that the Spaniards were unable to hold the Indians to preach the faith to them and instruct them in it, and that because of their great freedom the Indians fled and shunned the company of Christians ... although he did not have any more concern ... over what pertained to the salvation of the Indians than if they had been dogs or cats. ...

In view, then, of the eagerness and zeal Her Highness always had for all those peoples to receive the knowledge and faith of Jesus Christ, God, and Man, to become Christians and to be

saved, she answered him thus, saying among other things the
following:

"And since we desire the said Indians to be converted to our
holy Catholic faith ... and since that will be better brought
about by the said Indians' communicating with the Christians
... I order you our governor to henceforth, from the day you
see my letter, urge and compel the said Indians to confer and
to live with the Christians in the said island and to work in their
buildings, collecting gold and other metals, and providing sus-
tenance and profits for the Christian inhabitants of the said
island. And have each one paid a daily wage and maintenance
for the days he works ...

"Order each cacique who has charge of a certain number of
Indians to make them go work where they will be needed; and
command that on feast days and other days that seem appropriate, they come together to listen and be instructed in matters
of faith, in the places assigned. Order each cacique to turn out
with the number of Indians you prescribe to the person or persons you name, so that the Indians will labor at whatever such
persons command them to, paying them the daily wages fixed
by you.

"Let them do and discharge this as free persons, which they
are, and not as slaves; and let the said Indians be treated well,
and those who become Christians treated better than the others;
and do not consent or give an opportunity for any person to
injure them. ...." These are Her Highness' precise words, in
which she seems clearly to command and require eight things.

First ... the conversion of those peoples. ... Second that
each cacique should designate a certain number of his people
to go and hire themselves out to the Christians for a daily wage,
but that this number must include certain Indians, not all, and
... not women, nor children, nor old people, nor their leaders
and lords; and that some should go at one time and others at
another. ...

Third, that their needs had to be considered and those of
their wives and children ... so that each night they should go
to rest in their houses, or at least on Saturdays. Fourth, that
there had to be some time for work, but not all the time. ...
And that they had to be persuaded gently to do this willingly;

although Her Highness said "urge and compel them," it was understood as free men are accustomed to be compelled. Fifth, that their tasks had to be moderate and what they could endure, and performed on workdays, not on Sundays or feast days. . . .

Sixth, that the daily wage which they must be paid should be suitable and consistent with their labors. . . . Seventh, that the Indians were free and that they should do work as free persons, which they were, not as slaves, which they were not. . . . And eighth, that if that system and method which Her Highness ordered to be arranged . . . was impossible and so pernicious that it could not be or be endured without the total destruction of the Indians . . . they would not have to bear it, nor consent to remain a single day under such oppression in order to give the Christians gold.

Las Casas shows in detail that in the encomiendas which were established none of these "eight things" was carried out. In the History *of the Indies, Book II, Chapters 11-14, he expands this attack on the encomiendas of Nicolás de Ovando.*

[Conclusion]

Spaniards who hold Indians in encomiendas and wish to keep them as vassals usually . . . say and argue . . . that if the Indians are taken away from them the Spaniards will be unable to live in the land. They say that if the Indians remain by themselves, Your Majesty's dominion over them and, consequently, the Catholic faith, would be endangered . . . and they would go to hell as they were accustomed to before the Christians entered among them, etc. . . .

But to be good Christians, all should feel that even though it were possible for Your Majesty to lose his entire royal dominion and for the Indians never to become Christians, if the opposite could not take place without their death and total destruction, as has happened until now, it would not be unfitting for Your

Majesty to cease to be their lord and for them never to become Christians.

The reason is what has been given, because the law of Christians forbids that evil be done in order that good may follow.

❧{ 25 }❧

The Duty of Reparation

As bishop of Chiapa, Las Casas preached repentance and restitution to his hostile Spanish congregation. He instructed his priests not to give absolution to Spaniards who held Indians as slaves or profited from their labor in encomiendas; absolution was not to be given until the Spaniards freed the Indians and restored their ill-gotten gains. When he was in Mexico City in 1546, he wrote a Confesionario *("Twelve Rules for Confessors") to guide the clergy in his diocese in hearing confessions.*

The Confesionario *was supposed to circulate in private, but knowledge of its contents reached the public. Thereupon, the encomenderos brought a new and dangerous charge against Las Casas: that by denouncing the Spanish exploitation of the Indies he was, in effect, denying the legality of the conquest and of the king's title. He was guilty of lese majesty, or treason.*

The following selection, from the Confesionario *(1546, published 1552), illustrates Las Casas' uncompromising attitude.* (Obras Escogidas, *V, 235-236, 238.*)

Here are contained certain notices and rules for confessors hearing the confessions of Spaniards who have, or have had, charge of Indians . . . , brought together by the bishop of Chiapa, Don Fray Bartolomé de las Casas, or Casaus, of the Order of St. Dominic.

159

[First Rule]

The first rule in this matter concerns three kinds of persons who may come to confess: these are conquistadors; or settlers who hold Indians in encomiendas and who by another name are called encomenderos; the third are merchants, not all merchants but those who carried arms and goods to the men who were conquering or warring on the Indians, thus becoming participants.

If it is a conquistador and he wishes to confess at the point of death, have him call a notary public, or king's clerk, before he begins his confession, and have the confessor, by a public act, determined and prescribe the following:

First, let the conquistador say and affirm that he, as a faithful Christian and one who desires to depart this life without offending God and with his conscience unburdened, in order to appear before the divine judge in a secure condition, chooses as confessor so and so, a priest, cleric, or religious of such and such an order; and to him he gives full power . . . in all matters that the confessor considers pertinent to his salvation. And that if for this end it should seem necessary to the said confessor to restore his entire estate to the Indians . . . without anything remaining for his heirs, the confessor can freely do it, just as the same sick man or penitent could and should freely have done it in his lifetime. . . . And on this occasion he submits his entire estate to the judgment and sentence of his confessor, without any condition or limitation.

Second, let the notary public declare and set down that the penitent was found to have engaged in such and such conquests or wars against the Indians in these Indies; and that he carried out, and helped to carry out, thefts, violence, injuries, deaths, and captivities among them, as well as the destruction of many towns and villages. . . .

Third, let the notary public declare and set down that the penitent did not bring any estate from Castile, but that all he has was had from the Indians . . . and that another great estate added to his own would not suffice for satisfaction to the Indians. And therefore he desires, and it is his last wish, that the said confessor restore it to the Indians and make complete satisfaction for everything, at least as far as his entire estate will serve. And to that his conscience strictly enjoins him.

Fourth, if he possessed or possesses any Indians as slaves, under any title whatever, let him free them immediately and irrevocably, without any limitation or condition. And let him ask their pardon for the wrong he did them in enslaving, or helping to enslave, them, thus usurping their liberty. Or if he did not do this, for having bought, held, and profited from them as slaves, in bad faith. For this is certain, and let the confessor understand it: that there is no Spaniard in the Indies who has shown good faith in connection with the wars of conquest. . . .

Fifth, let him revoke any other testament or codicil he has made, affirming that he desires only this one to be valid and unchanged, and that it is to be executed as his last wish. And if necessary, he also gives the confessor power to implement this, for the sake of the said restitution and satisfaction, with any article or articles which the confessor considers fitting for the salvation of his soul.

[Fifth Rule]

The fifth rule: if the penitent is not in danger of death but confesses in good health, the confessor ought to meet with him and ask him, before the confession, if he wishes to escape from all doubt and render his conscience secure. And if he answers yes, with all his heart, let the confessor order the penitent to prepare a public contract by which he binds himself to abide by what the confessor will arrange for his entire estate and will consider fitting for his conscience, even though that be to expend all . . . And let him obligate all his goods in the same way as is described in the first rule.

This rule, along with the first, is clearly and formally justified in the same words, in the chapter *Super eo. de raptoribus*, where it is decreed by Pope Eugenius III that confessors cannot give absolution to robbers, which is what all the said conquistadors of the Indies are, unless they first return all they have stolen.

❧ 26 ❧

A Defense of Human Sacrifice

For his debate with Juan Ginés de Sepúlveda on the lawfulness of the Spanish conquest of the New World (see p. 13), Las Casas wrote a long Defense *in Latin. In it he refuted the argument that war against the Indians was justified because of their sins—war was a greater evil than the sins it was supposed to stamp out, said Las Casas. He defended the Indians against the charge that they were "slaves by nature" who should be ruled by others, and he even had the audacity to find reasons for their practice of human sacrifice.*

Like other sixteenth-century scholastics, Las Casas debated, armed with a wealth of citations from authorities—Church Fathers, later theologians, Roman and canon law. In fact, the Defense, *which until recently was available only in manuscript, gives a valuable picture of Las Casas in action at court as "Protector of the Indians," as well as a comprehensive view of his thought.*

The following selection, Chapter 34 of the Defense *(1550), develops an unusual excuse for the Indians through Aristotle's theory of "probable" error.*

From Bartolomé de Las Casas, *Defense Against the Persecutors and Slanderers of the Peoples of the New World Discovered across the Ocean*, ed. Ernest J. Burrus, S. J., trans. Stafford Poole, C. M. (Madrid: Series José Porrua Turanza; Editorial José Porruta Venero, 1971). Reprinted by permission of Father Stafford Poole.

We have come to the same conclusion [that we cannot punish the crimes of unbelievers] regarding the crime of human sacrifice, which is said to be one of their practices. It would not be right to make war on them for this reason both because ... it is difficult for them to absorb in a short time the truth proclaimed to them through messengers and also because the Indians are under no obligation to believe the Spaniards, even if they force the truth on them a thousand times. Why will they believe such a proud, greedy, cruel, and rapacious nation? Why will they give up the religion of their ancestors, unanimously approved for so many centuries and supported by the authority of their teachers, on the basis of a warning from a people whose words work no miracles to confirm the faith or lessen vice?

Even though the Indians cannot be excused in the sight of God for worshiping idols, yet they can be excused completely in the sight of men for two reasons. First, they are following a "probable" error for, as the Philosopher [Aristotle] notes, *Topics*, Book 1, something is said to be "probable" which is approved by all men, either by the majority of wise men or by those whose wisdom has the greatest following. Further, he says, *Rhetoric*, Book I, Chapter 20, "That must necessarily be judged to be good or better which is so judged by all, or the majority of men of good judgment or by those who are thought to have better judgment, even if only one person is forming the judgment." Judgments of this type, approved by the opinions of such men, are called morally certain, according to the same Philosopher whom all philosophers and theologians follow, *Ethics*, Book I, Chapter 2. Convictions about the gods, the duty of offering sacrifice to them, and the manner and thing to be sacrificed are fully agreed on by all the known Indian nations, and these gods are worshiped by those reputed to be sacred and holy men (that is, their priests), and their idolatry is established by the decrees of their laws, the sanctions of their rulers, and the penalties leveled against transgressors. Finally, since idols are not worshiped secretly, but publicly and religiously in their temples — and this from the earliest centuries — it is quite clear that the error of these people definitely is probable. Nor should we be surprised if they do not immediately arouse themselves at our first preaching.

Also, they are definitely in probable error about their practice of human sacrifice, since the ancient history of both pagans and Catholics testifies that almost all peoples used to do the same thing. For this is what Eusebius says, *De Praeparatione Evangelica*, Book IV, Chapter 7:

> It was common for all men, on the day customarily set for human sacrifice, to sprinkle the altar with human blood. This was the practice in ancient times when calamity or danger threatened. The ruler of the city or nation would offer to the avenging demon his favorite child as a ransom for the redemption of the whole people, and the one chosen would be slain in a mystic rite.

He goes on:

> Human sacrifice is demanded by the demons, who from time to time afflict many cities and nations with plagues and sudden calamities and ceaselessly harass the people in frightful ways until appeased by the blood of the victims offered them.

Again, Clement says, *Recognitiones ad Jacobum, Fratrem Domini*, Book IX, that some of the peoples of western India, who possibly were much like those we are dealing with, used to sacrifice foreigners to their gods and then devour them. Eusebius writes the same thing in the work which we have already quoted. In addition, Lactantius says, *De Divinis Institutionibus*, Book I, Chapter 21:

> Among the Tauri, an inhuman and savage nation, there was a law that a stranger should be sacrificed to Diana and such a sacrifice was offered for a long time. The Gauls placated Esus and Teutates with human blood. Even the Latins were not free of such barbarism. Indeed, even now the Jupiter of Latium is worshiped with human blood. . . . However, we should not be astonished at the barbarians whose religion matches their morals. Are not our own people, who boast of their meekness and gentleness, often

more inhuman than those who practice such sacrilegious rites?

Further on he notes, "It is now evident that this practice of human sacrifice is very ancient, for in honor of Saturn people used to be thrown into the Tiber from the Mulvian Bridge." And in regard to innocent children, he says:

I find no words to tell of the children who were sacrificed to the same Saturn out of hatred for Jupiter. Men were so barbarous and so inhuman that they labeled as sacrifice that foul and detestable crime against the human race which is parricide when, without any sign of family love, they blotted out tender and innocent lives at an age which is especially dear to parents. . . .

And later:

The Carthaginians had the custom of offering human sacrifice to Saturn, and when they were conquered by Aglothocles, king of Sicily, they made peace with their god who was angry with them, and so, in order that they might better discharge their guilt-offerings, they sacrificed 200 children from noble families.

Plutarch writes, *Problemata*, that the Romans failed to punish some barbarians who were sacrificing men to the gods because they knew that it was done out of custom and law. Plutarch also says that the Romans themselves did the same thing at times. Here are his own words:

When the Romans discovered that certain barbarians had sacrificed a man to their immortal gods, the magistrates thought that they should be summoned and punished. Later they released them when they learned that the barbarians did this because of a certain law and custom, and so they forbade them to do it again. This was because a few years before they themselves had buried [alive] two men and two women in the *Forum Boarium* at Rome. It

does not seem right that they should do this and yet find
fault with the savages who did the same. Were they persuaded that to offer a man to the immortal gods was evil
but to offer him to the demons was a necessity? Did they
think that those who did this sort of thing from custom
and law committed sin, while they believed that by following the command of the Sibylline books, they were not
guilty of the same crime?

The Greek historian Herodotus tells us, Book IV, that the
Scythians had the custom of sacrificing to their gods one out of
every hundred prisoners of war. He also maintains that the Scy-
tho-Tauri of Germany sacrifice everyone who is shipwrecked on
their shores, as well as strangers, to Iphigenia, the daughter of
Agamemnon. The same thing is recorded by Solinus, *Polyhisto-
ria*, Chapter 20, and Pomponius Mela, Book II, Chapter 1. Diodorus of Sicily writes, Book VI, that the Gauls sacrificed to their
gods captives or those condemned for their crimes. Strabo
reminds us, *De Situ Orbis*, Book III, that our own Spanish people, who reproach the poor Indians for human sacrifice, used to
sacrifice captives and their horses. He says that they forced some
to live next to the Duero River in a spartan manner. He continues:

Those who are given to sacrifice also practice divination
with entrails, especially those of captives. They cut off the
right hands of their victims and offer them to the gods.
They eat a goat which they sacrifice to Mars, as they do
with prisoners and horses.

Moreover, similar practices of other peoples are narrated in
other of Strabo's works. Polydore Vergil, *De Rerum Inventoribus*,
Book V, Chapter 8, has also recorded many similar details worth
remembering.

Since, then, human sacrifice to the gods has been customary
among so many different peoples, surely the Indians, in per-
forming human sacrifice for many centuries, are in probable
error.

We know that famous philosophers have lived in many parts

of the world. According to Augustine, *De Civitate Dei*, Book VI, Chapter 10, even though they know the stories about the gods to be fables and judged them to be undeserving of divine honors (this group includes Cicero and Seneca), they did not wish to turn the people from an ancient custom accepted for so many centuries. Why, then, should it be thought that at the words of Christian soldiers [who surpass the barbarous peoples in their wicked deeds], the Indians ought to turn from a religion which has been accepted for many centuries, sanctioned by the laws of many rulers, and strengthened by the example of so many prudent men? As Chrysostom says, *Homilia VIIa in Epistolam* ia *ad Corinthios*, in matters that are sacred and of great importance and very difficult to give up, they would be fickle and worthy of reproach and punishment if they put aside the many and great testimonies of such great authority and believe these soldiers in this matter, without being convinced by more probable reasons — and this cannot be done in a short time — that the Christian religion is more worthy of belief.

They ought to be ashamed who think to spread the gospel by means of the mailed fist. Men want to be taught, not forced. There is no way for our religion to be taught in a short time to those who are as ignorant of our language as we are of their language and religion, up to the point that those who prudently hold fast [to these beliefs] are convinced by reason. For, as we have said, there is no greater or more arduous step than for a man to abandon the religion which he has once embraced.

The Restoration of the Indies

When Las Casas was in his early eighties, he blocked an attempt of Spaniards in Peru to have their encomiendas made perpetual. He did this by his outspoken Letter to Carranza (Fray Bartolomé Miranda de Carranza, Philip II's confessor), which caused Philip II to indefinitely delay a decision about the encomiendas even though the colonists were offering him between 7 and 9 million ducats for the favor (see p. 14).

In the Letter, labeled a "little book" by one copyist, Las Casas arrived at his most extreme conclusions. To make up for past injustices, the Spaniards must free all Indians, subject the caciques only to a token tribute, and—except for a minimum number of paid garrisons to maintain the emperor's overlordship—withdraw from the Indies! The following selection, from the Letter to Carranza (August 1555), contains these extreme recommendations. (Obras Escogidas, V, 444-449.)

[A Token Tribute]

In the fifth supposition, Your Fathership says that the king of Castile must be recognized as supreme lord of all the new-found Indies, in order to establish and preserve the Christian religion, and for this they must give him his stipend, just as they gave it to Montezuma or to another lord. As for the first part of this supposition, I say, Father, that the king of Castile must be recognized in the new-found Indies as supreme prince and emperor over many kings only after the kings and natural lords of those realms, and their subjects the Indians, have been converted to the faith and made Christians of their own will, and not through force or violence. . . .

As for the second part, about the stipend as Your Fathership says, what I . . . think . . . is that, assuming that the above-mentioned preeminence of the kings of Castile is useful and profitable to the kings of the Indies and to their kingdoms, these kings, in order to acknowledge the preeminence, universal princedom, and dominion of the kings of Castile over them, may do so fully by a single jewel brought to the kings of Castile each year. Just so, the king of Tunis remained the emperor's vassal by providing him with certain horses or jewels every year. . . .

And if the kings of the Indies wish to assign the kings of Castile the claim and dominion they have over gold and silver mines, pearls, precious stones, and salt pits . . . , they will do our kings an outstanding service. If these mines, miners, and salt pits are granted our kings by the kings of the Indies, not one maravedi more of service may justly be taken from them or from their Indian subjects against their will. Clearly, I believe, the revenues and services owed Montezuma or other kings and caciques cannot be taken away, nor can Indian subjects be injured by being given two burdens; and the kings of the Indies may fairly reserve certain mines they prefer for themselves. . . .

When the said mines are granted to the kings of Castile, and also the duties and fees . . . which the Spaniards pay on their goods . . . and a thousand other profits which they . . . will have from those lands of the Indians, the kings of Castile will be sufficiently recompensed for their care in introducing and preserving the faith in those kingdoms of the Indies. For it is not reasonable, nor does Jesus Christ seek it by his law, that the Indians should be informed of the faith at a dearer rate than it was preached and made known to any other race in the world, and to us of Castile.

The expenses which the kings of Castile undergo in appointing audiencias, viceroys, governors, and other ministers of justice they do not undergo, Father, because of the Indians, who are

peaceful and very gentle. For one governor in 500 leagues is
more than enough for the Indians, who must be ruled not by
the justices of the king, but by their own kings and caciques. . . .
Thus, the kings of Castile are forced to appoint audiencias, viceroys, and many other justices not for the Indians but for the
Spaniards, who never live quietly without quarrels and lawsuits,
injuring one another. . . . These must also be appointed . . . to
defend the Indians from the Spaniards. . . . Therefore, the kings
.of Castile have a great obligation to provide the said justices at
their own expense and not at that of the Indians, any more than
has been said.

[Indian Self-Government]

To the sixth supposition of Your Fathership, which states that
the Spaniards are necessary for the Indians and for their good
way of life, especially for their religion, I say . . . would to God
that, in temporal affairs, Spain had been as well governed as the
Indies and had such a good way of life!

Where throughout the inhabited world were there greater
populations . . . than in the Indies? The great City of Mexico
. . . had over 200,000 residents; and in Tlascala, Mechuacán,
Tepeaca, Tezcuco, and an infinite number of other cities in New
Spain and Guatemala, in the city of Cuzco, and in all parts of
the Indies, . . . there were many millions of people. . . . When
we entered there . . . would we have found such great unions of
peoples in their towns and cities if they had lacked the order of
a good way of life, peace, concord, and justice? No republic or
city can be preserved or can last, nor can a multitude of men
live together, without the said virtues, as is apparent from the
Philosopher's [Aristotle's] *Ethics* and *Politics*, and as is manifest
to every prudent man.

Therefore, Father, the Indians have no need of Spaniards for
their good way of life; thus, to say . . . that the Indians need
them for that—what else is this but an excuse and feigned pretext to rob and oppress the Indians, to keep them in servitude,
and to hold them in encomiendas and under Spanish despotism?

Truly, I say to Your Fathership that to ... restore the Indians to their human and temporal good way of life, not a single Spaniard would have to remain in the Indies. For who has disturbed, disordered, and completely annihilated the good way of life of the Indians—insofar as pagans are capable of a good way of life—but the Spaniards? ... Therefore, Father, do not lend your ears to such falsehood and wickedness.

As for religion, I say also that if it were possible to distinguish and sort out this contradiction of the Spaniards' being and not being in the Indies—being there to maintain the preeminence and sovereign lordship of the kings of Castile, and not being there so as not to impede and pervert the religion of Christ by their corrupt works and fatal examples—I affirm before Jesus Christ that it would be necessary, and the best thing imaginable, to cast them all out, except a few chosen ones, so that the Indians could receive the faith.

[Fewer Spaniards]

The only need that remains, then, for Spaniards in the Indies is to assert and preserve there the princedom, sovereign dominion, and universal jurisdiction of the kings of Castile. ... To support that dominion and preeminence it is not required, nor is it necessary, that the thousands of Spaniards now itching to leave Castile should go to the Indies or remain there. For that purpose it suffices that in each kingdom there should be three or four towns ... depending on the territory and the number of Indian settlements such a kingdom contains.

Guatemala is a kingdom seventy or eighty leagues square and has a large number of Indian towns, but has in all only three towns of Spaniards. The city of Santiago has a little more than one hundred inhabitants; San Salvador, fifty, and San Miguel, thirty; I even believe they do not exceed twenty-five. The kingdom of Chiapa covers almost as many leagues, and contains only the city of Chiapa, which will come to fifty inhabitants; I even believe, not that many.

Few armies are necessary to maintain peace among a naked

people, clad only in skins, Father, and without any weapons, especially a race as humble and mild by nature as the Indians. The kings of Castile should give these Spaniards, who will not be, nor need be, numerous . . . a certain part of their income from gold, silver, and other things . . . ; but the Indians are not obliged to give them anything.

Let there be placed in Mexico a garrison of 300 men, whom the king gives 200 or 300 ducats each year, as well as land, forests, waters, and other things which can be conferred without injury to the Indians . . . not in perpetuity, but temporarily. . . . And after this garrison is established, let all the Indians be set free; and because of their joy over this they will serve the king with their blood, if necessary, and will give him 2 or 3 millions.

When they are deprived of their Indians, some Spaniards who are already rich are bound to want to come to Castile. And they will sell their estates — because they can't bring them with them — and others who wish to remain without making a change will be certain to buy them. Thus the land will be peopled simply through the king's having this garrison there, which makes him lord of it.

And these 300 men will not have just the 200 or 300 pesos or ducats which the king gives them, because conditions there are not as they are here. . . . For there, with no more pesos or ducats than these, one can undertake a thousand profitable enterprises in lands, plantings, and merchandise, whence men with small means become rich because of the fertility of the earth. These men alone will suffice to secure the lands from the beginning of New Spain to Nicaragua, which is 500 leagues.

In Peru, once those tyrants and traitors are subjugated by means of war or in some other way, 500 men must be stationed. And those will be sufficient for all that land, which the Spaniards have settled, or, better say, destroyed, where they live. This, Father, is the true and prime way for the kings of Castile to be lords of the Indies and to be able to extricate them from tyranny. . . . Thus the land will endure.

[No Perpetual Encomiendas]

From what has been said, the response to the seventh and last supposition of Your Fathership seems clear: that is, that there is no way except a diabolical and pernicious one, condemned by every law and degree of reason, to give a single encomienda, in perpetuity or temporarily, even if it were only for one hour. For to do this is to deprive the Indians of their liberty, and their kings and lords of their dominions, with all the other hideous consequences described above. In short, it is nothing other than to hand them over to madmen who have sharp knives in their hands, and therefore neither king nor pope has any more power than a private person to do this.

❖{ 28 }❖

A Declaration of Human Rights

In all his writings, Las Casas defends the rationality of the Indians and argues that all men are equal in their human dignity and their potentiality for development through educa-tion. The following selection, from Chapter 48 of the Apolo-getic History, *sums up this Christian and humanitarian belief of Las Casas.* (Obras Escogidas *III, 165-166.*)

[All the Races of the World Are Men]

From these examples, ancient and modern, it clearly appears that there are no races in the world, however rude, uncultivated, barbarous, gross, or almost brutal they may be, who cannot be persuaded and brought to a good order and way of life, and made domestic, mild, and tractable, provided ... the method that is proper and natural to men is used; that is, love and gentleness and kindness. ...

The reason for this truth is—and Cicero sets it down in *De Legibus*, Book I—that all the races of the world are men, and of all men and of each individual there is but one definition, and this is that they are rational. All have understanding and will and free choice, as all are made in the image and likeness of God.

All men possess five exterior and four interior senses, and are moved by the same objects of those senses. All have motives

174

implanted by nature for understanding, learning, and knowing the sciences and other things which they do not know; and not only is this true of the well-inclined, but these motives are also found in those who, because of depraved customs, are evil. All take satisfaction in the good and experience pleasure from what is delightful and festive; and all repudiate and detest evil, and change because of what is hard or what does them injury.

[A Quotation from Cicero]

In fact, there is no human being of any race who, if he uses nature as a guide, cannot attain to virtue. The similarity of the human race is clearly marked in its evil tendencies as well as in its goodness. For pleasure also attracts all men; and even though it is an enticement to vice, yet it has some likeness to what is naturally good, by its lightness and agreeableness.

And below:

But what nation does not love courtesy, kindliness, gratitude, and remembrance of favors bestowed? What people does not hate and despise the haughty, the wicked, the cruel, and the ungrateful? Inasmuch as these considerations prove to us that the whole human race is bound together in unity, it follows, finally, that knowledge of the principles of right living is what makes men better, etc.

All this is from Cicero.

[The Equality of Man]

Thus the entire human race is one; all men are alike with respect to their creation and the things of nature, and none is born already taught. And so we all have the need, from the beginning, to be guided and helped by those who have been born earlier.

Thus, when some very rustic peoples are found in the world, they are like untilled land, which easily produces worthless weeds and thorns, but has within itself so much natural power that when it is plowed and cultivated it gives useful and wholesome fruits.

All the races of the world have understanding and will and that which results from these two faculties in man — that is, free choice. And consequently, all have the power and ability or capacity . . . to be instructed, persuaded, and attracted to order and reason and laws and virtue and all goodness.

Bibliography

Editions of Las Casas' Works

Las Casas, Bartolomé de. *Apologética historia sumaria*, ed. Edmundo O'Gorman. 2 vols. México City: Universidad Nacional Autónoma, 1967.

———. *De regia potestate, o derecho de autodeterminación.* Ed. Luciano Pereña, J. M. Pérez Frendes, Vidal Abril, and Joaquín Azcarraga. (Corpus Hispanorum de Pace, v. 8) Madrid: Consejo Superior de Investigaciones Científicas, 1969.

———. *Del único modo de atraer a todos los pueblos a la verdadera religión*, ed. Agustín Millares Carlo. México City: Fondo de Cultura Económica, 1942.

———. *Historia de las Indias*, ed. Augustín Millares Carlo. 3 vols. México City: Fondo de Cultura Económica, 1951.

———. *In Defense of the Indians: The Defense of . . . [Las Casas] Against the Persecutors and Slanderers of the People of the New World Discovered Across the Sea.* Trans., ed., and annotated by Stafford Poole. DeKalb, Ill.: Northern Illinois University Press, 1974.

———. *Obras escogidas*, ed. Juan Pérez de Tudela. 5 vols. Madrid: Biblioteca de Autores Españoles; v. 95-96, *Historia de las Indias*; v. 105-106, *Apologética Historia*; v. 110, *Opusculos, cartas, y memoriales.* 1957-1958.

———. *Los tesoros del Perú.* Ed. Angel Losada. Madrid: Consejo Superior de Investigaciones Científicas, 1958.

Bartolomé de las Casas: The Only Way, a new restored version, ed. Helen Rand Parish, trans. Francis Patrick Sullivan. Mahwah, NJ: Paulist Press, 1992.

Las Casas' pro-Indian Tracts. v. 1, *The New Laws.* Ed. by Helen Rand Parish, trans. by Francis Patrick Sullivan. (*The Decimation of the Indians*; *Twenty Reasons Against Encomienda*; *The Illegal Enslavement of the Indians.*) Kansas City, Missouri: Sheed & Ward, 1992 (forthcoming).

177

Bibliography, Catalog, Chronology

Hanke, Lewis, and Manuel Giménez Fernández. *Bartolomé de las Casas: 1474-1566. Bibliografía crítica.* Santiago de Chile: Fondo Histórico y Bibliográfico José Toribio Medina, 1954.

Hernández Ruigómez, Almudena and Carlos Ma., González de Heredia y de Añate, "Materiales para una bibliografía sobre Fray Bartolomé de Las Casas," in *En el Quinto Centenario de Bartolomé de las Casas,* Ediciones Cultura Hispanica, Instituto de Cooperación Iberoamericana (Madrid, 1989), pp. 183-231.

Pérez Fernández, Isacio, *Inventario documentado de los escritos de Fray Bartolomé de las Casas.* Rev. by Helen Rand Parish. Bayamón, Puerto Rico: Centro de Estudios de los dominicos del Caribe, 1981.

———. *Cronología documentada de los viajes, estancias y actuaciones de Fray Bartolomé de las Casas.* Bayamon, P.R.: CEDOC, Universidad Central de Bayamón, 1984.

Biographies, Ancient Chronicles, Modern Studies

Bataillon, Marcel. *Études sur Bartolomé de Las Casas,* ed. Raymond Marcus. Paris: Centre de Recherches de l'Institut d'Études Hispaniques, 1965.

Castro, Américo. *Fray Bartolomé de las Casas.* Paris: Centre de Recherches de l'Institut d'Études Hispaniques, 1965. Originally published in *Mélanges à la mémoire de Jean Sarrialh.*

Fabié, Antonio María. *Vida y escritos de don fray Bartolomé de Las Casas, obispo de Chiapa.* 2 vols. Madrid, 1879.

Fernández de Oviedo y Valdés, Gonzalo. *Historia general y natural de las Indias,* ed. Juan Pérez de Tudela. 5 vols. Madrid: Biblioteca de Autores Españoles, 1959.

Giménez Fernández, Manuel. *Bartolomé de Las Casas.* 2 vols. Seville: Escuela de Estudios hispaño-americanos, 1953, 1960.

———. *Breve biografía de Fray Bartolomé de Las Casas.* Seville: Universidad de Sevilla, 1966.

Hanke, Lewis. *All Mankind Is One: A Study of the Disputation between Bartolomé de las Casas and Juan Ginés de Sepúlveda in 1550 on the Intellectual and Religious Capacity of the American Indians.* (Introductory volume for Stafford Poole's trans. of Las Casas' *In Defense of the Indians.*) DeKalb, Illinois: Northern Illinois University Press, 1974.

———. *Bartolomé de Las Casas.* The Hague: Martinus Nijhoff, 1951.

———. *Bartolomé de Las Casas: Historian.* Gainesville: University of Florida Press, 1952.

———. *Bartolomé de Las Casas: Pensador politico, historiador, antropólogo.* Havana: Sociedad Económica de Amigos del Pais, 1949.

———. *Estudios sobre Fray Bartolomé de Las Casas y sobre la lucha por la justicia en la conquista española de América.* Caracas: Universidad Central de Venezuela, 1968.

———. *The First Social Experiments in America.* Cambridge: Harvard University Press, 1935.

———. *The Spanish Struggle for Justice in the Conquest of America.* Boston: Little, Brown, 1965; first printed 1949.

Keen, Benjamin and Juan Friede. *Bartolomé de Las Casas in History.* DeKalb, Illinois: Northern Illinois University Press, 1971.

Martínez, Manuel María. *Fray Bartolomé de Las Casas: El gran caluminiado.* Madrid, 1955.

Motolinía, Fray Toribio de. "Carta al Emperador" in *Documentos inéditos de América*, VII, 254-289.

O'Gorman, Edmundo. "Estudio preliminar" in Bartolomé de Las Casas, *Apologética historia sumaria*, ed. Edmundo O'Gorman, I, xv-lxxix. México City: Universidad Nacional Autónoma, 1967.

———. *La idea del descubrimiento de América.* México City: Universidad Nacional Autónoma, 1951.

———. *The Invention of America.* Bloomington: Indiana University Press, 1961.

Parish, Helen Rand. *Las Casas as a Bishop: A New Interpretation Based on His Holograph Petition . . . /Las Casas, Obispo: . . .* Washington: Library of Congress, 1980.

———. "Las Casas' Spirituality—The Three Crises," Introduction to *Bartolomé de las Casas: The Only Way*, ed. Parish, pp. 1-58, and Addenda, pp. 185-208. Mahwah, NJ: Paulist Press, 1992.

———. "The Secret Inside Story of Las Casas and the New Laws," Introduction to *Las Casas' pro-Indian Tracts*, v. 1, ed. Parish.

Parish, Helen Rand, ed. *The Royal File on the administration of the Indians* (in press)/ *La Carpeta Real sobre la administración de los indios* (in preparation). Washington: Library of Congress, 1991.

Parish, Helen Rand with Harold E. Weidman, "The Correct Birthdate of Bartolomé de las Casas," *Hispanic American Historical Review*, v. 56, Aug. 1976: 385-406.

———. *Las Casas en México: Historia y obra desconocidas.* 2 vols. México City, Fondo de Cultura Económica, 1992 (forthcoming).

Pérez de Tudela, Juan. "Estudio crítico preliminar" in Bartolomé de Las Casas, *Obras escogidas*, ed. Pérez de Tudela, I, ix-clxxxvi. Madrid: Biblioteca de Autores Españoles, 1957-1958.

Pérez Fernández Isacio, *Bartolomé de las Casas contra los negros? Revi-*

sión de una levenda. Madrid: Editorial Mundo Negro; México: Ediciones Esquila. 1991.

Remesal, Antonio de. *Historia general de las Indias occidentales, y particular de la gobernación de Chiapa y Guatemala.* Madrid: Francisco de Ángulo, 1619.

Saint-Lu, André. *La Vera Paz, Esprit Évangelique et Colonisation.* Paris: Centre de Recherches Hispaniques de l'Institut d'Études Hispaniques, 1968.

Simpson, Lesley Byrd. *The Encomienda in New Spain.* Berkeley: University of California Press, 1950.

Wagner, Henry Raup, and Helen Rand Parish. *The Life and Writing of Bartolomé de las Casas.* Albuquerque: University of New Mexico Press, 1967.

Yáñez, Agustín. *Fray Bartolomé de Las Casas: El conquistador conquistado.* México City: Xochitl, 1942.

———. *Fray Bartolomé de Las Casas: Doctrina.* México City: Universidad Nacional Autónoma, 1941.

Zavala, Silvio. *La encomienda indiana.* Madrid: Imprenta helénica, 1935.

———. *Estudios indianos.* México City: Colegio Nacional, 1948.

———. *New Viewpoints on the Spanish Colonization of America.* Philadelphia: University of Pennsylvania Press, 1943.

———. *Servidumbre natural y libertad cristiana, según los tratadistas españoles de los siglos XVI y XVII.* Buenos Aires: Instituto de Investigaciones Históricas, 1944.

Chronology

August 1484 Born in Seville

April 1493 Witnesses Columbus's return to Seville after first voyage to New World

January 1502 Embarks for Hispaniola with Nicolás de Ovando, as an eighteen-year-old colonist

1506-1507 Journeys to Rome, where he is ordained a priest

1512-1513 Accompanies Panfilo de Narváez as a chaplain in the Spanish conquest of Cuba

1514 Becomes convinced that the whole pattern of Spanish conquest and exploitation of the Indians is unjust, and resolves to change the system.

December 1515 Protests at court in Spain against Spanish mistreatment of the Indians and offers plans for peaceful acculturation

1516 Is appointed "Protector of the Indians"; his plans are the basis of instructions for the Jeronymite friars who are investigating Indian affairs

1518-1519 Attempts to recruit Spanish farmers to emigrate to the Indies

May 19, 1520 Obtains a grant of 260 leagues of the coast of Venezuela for a colony

1520-1522 Fails in his attempted colony because Spanish slave raiders provoke an Indian revolt

December 1522 Enters the Dominican Order in Hispaniola

1527 Founds a Dominican monastery in Puerto de Plata, Hispaniola; begins the *History of the Indies* here

January 1534 Pacifies the Indian rebel Enriquillo, who had defied
Spanish authorities of Hispaniola

1534 Writes *The Only Method of Attracting All People to
the True Faith*

1535-1536 Denounces an expedition of conquest in Nicaragua,
under Rodrigo de Contreras and gets it postponed

1537-1539 Organizes a Dominican mission which begins the
conversion of Tuzulutlán, Guatemala — "The
Land of War"

1540-1543 Campaigns at the Spanish court for the New Laws;
writes the *Very Brief Account of the Destruction of
the Indies*

March 30, 1544 Is consecrated bishop of Chiapa, Mexico

1545 Arrives in Chiapa and encounters rebellion of his
Spanish flock against obeying laws on the encomienda and Indian slavery

1546 Attends conference of New Spain bishops in Mexico
City; promotes friars' conference, which con-
demns Indian slavery; writes his *Confesionario*

1547-1549 Returns to Spain and takes up permanent residence
at court; strengthens remaining New Laws

1550-1551 Debates the justice of the Spanish conquest with
Ginés de Sepúlveda before a royal commission

August 1550 Resigns the bishopric of Chiapa

1552 Has eight treatises printed in Seville, including the
Very Brief Account of the Destruction of the Indies

1554-1560 Defeats an attempt of the conquistadors of Peru to
have their encomiendas made perpetual

1559 Completes the *Apologetic History*

1562-1564 Revises the *History of the Indies*, Books I-III

July 18, 1566 Dies in a Dominican monastery in Madrid